Robert Rando & Caroline Scutt

FRENCHTOWN NEW JERSEY

History Along the River

THE History PRESS

Published by The History Press
Charleston, SC 29403
www.historypress.net

First published 2015

Manufactured in the United States

ISBN 978.1.62619.711.4

Library of Congress Control Number: 2015934346

CONTENTS

FOREWORD

Frenchtown is a magical place. Slightly more than one mile square, it is home to fewer than 1,400 residents—fewer than live in a single building in some cities. Outsiders sometimes call the borough Mayberry, after Andy Griffith's 1960s television town. We don't mind. We sometimes call it Mayberry ourselves.

The main part of the town, "downtown" and "the numbered streets" (there are just twelve, with alleys running between backyards), tucks into the Delaware River. An old iron truss bridge spans the river, and five roads start or end here, depending on your point of view. The truth is, it is hard to get anywhere in western Hunterdon County without passing through Frenchtown. According to the chief of our five-man police department (Chief Al, two full timers and two part timers), more than five thousand cars travel across the bridge every day, and a similar number head in and out of town on each of the other roads as well, he'll tell you.

On nice weekends throughout the year, downtown sidewalks are crowded with visitors. They come to eat, shop or ride their bicycles on the former railroad bed that runs north–south through the Delaware and Raritan Canal State Park. In fine weather, people come to town to picnic. (Frenchtown is the only town in Hunterdon County where there's extensive public access to the river.) They also come to fish, kayak, float down the river in inner tubes or just sit and watch it flow by. Often, visitors return to Frenchtown to become residents. It's that kind of place.

In Frenchtown, almost everyone thinks they know almost everyone else…and it's mostly true. In many ways, Frenchtown reminds me of the

West Orange neighborhood I grew up in in the late 1950s and early '60s. If you got in trouble as a child in Pleasantdale (really!), your bicycle couldn't get you home fast enough to tell your mother your version of the story before she'd heard about it from several other parents.

In winter, when snow falls quickly and deeply in Frenchtown, families take to the streets, walking side by side to visit neighbors or shuffle over the snow-covered bridge to rural Bucks County, Pennsylvania. If it's cold enough long enough, volunteer firefighter Mike Atheras of Frenchtown's Union Fire Company will pump water from the Nishisackwick Creek into the "rink," an acre or so depression in Borough Park that was dug by hand more than thirty years ago by Harold Matthews, the town's one-man Parks Department in those days. It freezes solid over the course of a day or two and stays frozen—if we're lucky—long enough for children and adults alike to tie on skates and scrape around on the ice for a few hours or gather near the bonfire drinking hot chocolate.

Every New Year's Day, we'll meet at the bridge to watch fireworks set off across the river by Dr. Boom Bo Hahn, the retired optometrist who walks into Frenchtown from his Pennsylvania home nearly every day, sometimes with his dog. On Memorial Day, the mayor speaks about war and peace and patriotism in front of the American Legion Hall, and then a parade led by the honor guard in their white spats and the school band in their blue uniforms and gold-braided caps flows through the center of town to the Union Cemetery, where the pastor of the Frenchtown Presbyterian Church on Fourth Street (there are churches on Second and Third Streets too) leads a prayer for the town's veterans, those passed and those still living.

During Riverfest, we gather at the end of Harrison Street to judge the annual pet parade. At Halloween, costumed children (and no small number of adults) pass the reviewing stand at the American Legion and afterward line up inside for hot dogs and brownies. In December, we light a Christmas tree and a Chanukah menorah, caroling one night and singing about latkes another.

Frenchtown is chiefly a friendly place, though I've heard that there are one or two who don't care for dogs or children. We have more than our share of characters. Frenchtown poet Skye Van Saun likes to say about us: "We're all here because we're not all there." It's the only place I know where children say hello to old folks—and say their names. In our small downtown, there are those among us who patronize Galasso's Pizzeria and others who favor Napoli's. There's a tattoo studio, a drugstore, a bicycle shop, a bookstore and an old-fashioned candy store. Artists' galleries come and go and come again.

Foreword

Ron Kobi has been selling carved decoys and wildlife paintings on Bridge Street for—well, nobody knows how long. Other than the gas station and the bank, there are no brand names here. People in town still call the corner store at Bridge and Race Streets Schiable's after the deceased barber who gave three generations of Frenchtown men their first haircuts as they sat in Philadelphia Eagles' football helmet barber chairs on the verge of tears.

Frenchtown has artists and writers, musicians and actors, artisans, plumbers, electricians and house painters. It's home to doctors and lawyers and master gardeners and teachers and cooks. We are gay, straight, black, white, Christian, Muslim and Jew. There's a yoga studio and a florist shop and lots of eateries and boutiques. In the Frenchtown Launderette, a mural of garments on a clothesline has adorned the wall above the dryers for nearly twenty years. (My then eight-year-old son painted the bra.) Some celebrities call Frenchtown home, as do some folks who'd be anonymous elsewhere. (It's hard to be anonymous in Frenchtown.) In front of the elementary school stands a statue of a charging World War I doughboy holding a hand grenade. We are a blue-collar town that occasionally wears a tie—and secretly a tie-dyed T-shirt. Many of us have tattoos. Some of us raise chickens. Few of us put on airs…I can't imagine living anywhere else.

Warren Cooper, mayor of Frenchtown

ACKNOWLEDGEMENTS

First, we need to thank everyone who walked through the doors of The Book Garden enquiring about a written history of Frenchtown. Those constant requests led us on this path of exploration and publication.

Frenchtown is a remarkable community with a rich history and a promising future. We are honored to have been asked to capture a snapshot of the Frenchtown story and would like to thank everyone who contributed to this book, as the story would have been lacking without their help. First, thank you to the team at The History Press, especially our commissioning editor, Whitney Landis, for helping us bring this book to life.

Thank you to photographer Bill Brokaw, who provided the majority of the modern-day photos, and to Rick Epstein, David Miller and Robert Trimmer for sharing their libraries of snapshots and other memorabilia depicting Frenchtown in the first half of the twentieth century. Thanks also go to Robb Arent, who digitized many of the photographs. We also would like to thank John Schmidtberger for the use of his beautiful rendition of the Hummer Building on the cover and to all of the Frenchtown residents who agreed to be interviewed—so many wonderful stories that could fill volumes!

The authors are also indebted to Mayor Warren Cooper and Elizabeth Gilbert for beautifully framing the Frenchtown story with their personal sketches and to Ellen Fletcher for helping to put the gems of Frenchtown onto the National Register of Historic Places.

Lastly, we wish to acknowledge Clarence Fargo. If he had not captured Frenchtown's early history in his writings, many of the unique qualities of this little river town might have been lost. Fortunately for us all, Mr. Fargo made sure Frenchtown's story could continue to be told for generations to come.

INTRODUCTION

Welcome to Frenchtown

Travel back in time and walk along the shores of the majestic Delaware River when the Leni-Lenape Indians inhabited this quiet valley. Wander through the mill town when farmers' overflowing wagons stirred up the dust on Main Street before stopping to sell or trade their grain and livestock and then shop for goods at Riche's.

Visit Frenchtown when riverfront industries grew and drove business in the bustling downtown and again when shuttered factories and empty storefronts weren't enough to defeat this close-knit community. See a renaissance unfold as history continues to be made in this once-again vibrant river town.

This book presents a sliver of Frenchtown's rich history. Many places and persons were omitted, not because they weren't deemed important enough to include but because the authors were limited in time and space. As one resident, Stephanie Markert Haver, proudly points out, "If you were to draw Frenchtown's family tree, you would be amazed to see all the connections." Amazed we continue to be.

1

EARLY SETTLEMENT OF HUNTERDON COUNTY

1700s

Before the Europeans

To understand the personality of any town, one must study the make of the region before and well after the town itself was placed on the map. This study must encompass how the locality was molded, how ownership transfers were enacted and what constituted the underlying power struggles. In this regard, to begin to understand the founding and development of Frenchtown, New Jersey, one must first acknowledge the original peoples, the Native Americans and the emigrating clans of Europeans who, through economic or physical means, fought for ownership of the lands among themselves as well as among one another.

The Native Americans included the Iroquois (named by the French), who called themselves the Mengwes, and the Delaware tribes (named by the English), who called themselves the Leni-Lenapes. The Mengwes roamed most of the state of New York and parts of Canada. The five Mengwe nations were the Mohawks, Senecas, Cayugas, Onondagas and the Oneidas.

The Delawares roamed from the Chesapeake to Long Island Sound and west to the Susquehanna. This included all of the state of New Jersey. In their language, *Lenni Lenape* means "original people," a title they adopted

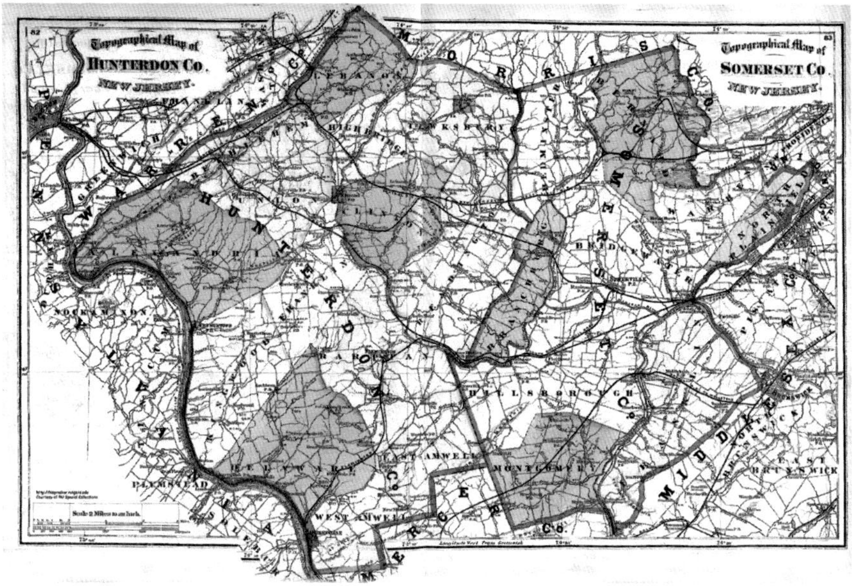

A fairly detailed map of Hunterdon and Somerset Counties, circa 1872, taken from James P. Snell's *History of Hunterdon & Somerset Counties* (1881).

under the claim they were descended from the most ancient of all Indian ancestry. Most Native Americans lived along the water (rivers, bays and oceans) because, simply put, they ate better that way and traveling was easier.

It does not appear as if Indians inhabiting the interior portions of New Jersey were numerous. A 1648 publication entitled *A Description of New Albion* stated that about twenty kings governed the native people in this section of the new lands, but the insignificance of the power of those "kings" is obvious from the accompanying statement:

> *There were twelve hundred* [Indians] *under the two Raritan Kings on the north side, next to Hudson's River, and those came down to the ocean about little Egg-bay and Sandy Barengatte; and about the South Cape two small kings of forty men apiece, and a third, reduce to fourteen men, at Roymount.*

William Whitehead, in his *East Jersey Under the Proprietary Governments*, concludes, "There were probably not more than two thousand [Indians] within the province while it was under the domination of the Dutch."

The first Europeans settled around the place that would become Frenchtown—at the confluence of the Nishisakawick (the old spelling is

Nickisakawick) Creek and the Delaware River—about the middle of the eighteenth century. Well before their arrival, the Leni-Lenapes roamed the river and its flood plain, hunting, fishing and planting crops according to the season. Old Indian fields, fishing grounds, campsites and trails often formed the underpinning for later European settlements, their patterns hinting at the most fertile spots, the easiest routes and river crossings and the most wind-sheltered sites for houses. It is likely that Frenchtown is built on the site of Leni-Lenape fields and that local roads once followed Native American pathways.

To understand the migratory flow of settlers and the establishment of settlements along the Delaware River, one must begin with Henry Hudson and the first European incursions into what is today New Jersey, New York and Pennsylvania. In 1609, the Dutch East India Company and Henry Hudson joined forces. This was not Hudson's first trip to the New World. In previous visits, he searched the northern climes for the Northwest Passage to China, and two years later, in 1611, he would return to these efforts and take his final voyage on which several points of interest now bear his name (e.g., Hudson Bay and the Straights of Hudson).

In 1609, Hudson boarded his boat, the *Halve-Maan* (*Half-Moon*), and took a more southerly route. On this voyage, the *Halve-Maan* first made landfall in Newfoundland before the ship moved south to the Penobscot region of what is now Maine, where it remained a week. There, the crew cut timber for a new foremast. Hudson and his crew then sailed south until they entered the Chesapeake Bay. The visit to the Chesapeake was short, and soon after, the *Halve-Maan* was anchored in the Delaware Bay. Again, Hudson only stayed in these waters for a short time before he proceeded along the coast northward, following the eastern shore of New Jersey. He finally anchored inside of Sandy Hook on September 3, 1609.

Hudson and his crew were not the first Europeans to arrive here. Giovanni da Verrazzano recorded his visit in 1524, but it was Hudson who sailed up the river that bears his name. Hudson's expedition sailed north to a point (according to his own account) at least fifty-three leagues from the river's mouth. Returning back down the river on October 4, Hudson proceeded directly back to Europe without anchoring in New York Bay.

Hudson's activities opened the door to settlement, which also opened the door to grabbing land. The Dutch now had an entryway into the heart of the American continent. It was these new lands where the best furs could be procured without interruption from the French or English, though both also laid claim to this territory. The Dutch were not slow in availing themselves of this golden opportunity.

Five years after Hudson's voyage, a company of merchants, under the permission of the States General of Holland and with exclusive rights to trade on Hudson's River, had built forts and established trading posts from New Amsterdam (New York) to Albany. By 1611, the company of merchants had received its special grant conferring on it the exclusive right to "visit and navigate all the lands situate in America between New France and Virginia." Having thus obtained the exclusive rights to trade in the new country, it assumed the name the United New Netherland Company.

The Hollanders were a trading people, and their bartering, or trading, posts were established at points that were natural outlets for all the trapping regions with tributaries to the Hudson. Those Dutch who followed, like the Walloons, founded the first permanent settlements beyond the immediate protection of the cannons of Fort Amsterdam. They settled in Brooklyn and were the first who professionally pursued agriculture. Danes and Norwegians accompanied the Dutch colonists to New Netherlands and had established a settlement at Bergan by 1618. By 1623, the West India Company was sending groups of settlers up both the Delaware and the Hudson Rivers.

MILL TOWN SETTLEMENTS AND PROPRIETARY GOVERNMENTS

Cornelius Jacobus Mey, for whom Cape May is named, commanded the first ship traveling up the Delaware. This group built a fortification (Fort Nassau) just below what is now Camden, but by 1630, this settlement no longer existed, having fallen due to a feud with one of the local native tribes. A similar fate was narrowly escaped by David Pietersen De Vries's expedition, and for a while, the Dutch became disheartened by these activities and pulled back from areas along the Delaware.

Shortly after the Dutch pulled back, the Swedish West India Company began to move in. In 1637, two Swedish ships embarked from the port of Gothenburg loaded with settlers. Shortly after arriving in the Delaware Bay, this expedition built Fort Christina near modern-day Wilmington, Delaware. Peter Minuit—the former governor of New Amsterdam and former director of the Dutch West India Company—led this expedition. Between 1638 and 1655, the Swedish West India Company bankrolled eleven different expeditions. Being familiar with the Dutch claim to holdings to the east of the Delaware River (New Jersey), Minuit planned to colonize areas to the west of this river in what today is Maryland, Delaware and Pennsylvania. Though appointed the first governor of New Sweden, Minuit died on a return trip to Sweden that very same year.

In 1642, a military officer named Johan Printz was assigned to expand the company holdings and govern the Swedish colony. Under his stewardship, forts were built on both sides of the Delaware to secure a monopoly of trade with the Indians as far north as modern-day Trenton. He also established the first recorded European settlement in Pennsylvania. The village was placed on the island known as Tinicum—or, as the Leni-Lenape would say, *Tin-eek Unk*—just to the south and west of where Philadelphia would be built. (Tinicum Township, Delaware County, Pennsylvania, is not to be confused with Tinicum Township, Bucks County, Pennsylvania, which is farther north and close to Frenchtown.) On Tinicum, Printz built Fort Nya Gothenborg, a church and several dwellings, which included his home Printzhof (Printz Hall). In 1643, he moved his capital from Fort Christina to Tinicum Island and, soon after, built Printz's Mill to help the farmers immigrating to New Sweden.

The success of New Sweden did not please political or business rivals. In 1655, Peter Stuyvesant, director-general of the New Netherland colony, sailed into the Delaware Bay with a fleet of seven vessels and about seven hundred men and systematically began to take possession of New Sweden. Fort after fort fell into Dutch hands, and the principals of New Sweden were soon transported back to New Amsterdam as prisoners. The Dutch now controlled both sides of the Delaware River (renaming this region New Amstel), but this was a short-lived victory.

In 1664, King Charles II of England ceded to his brother—the Duke of York, later King James II—a large tract of land that included New Netherland. The problem was that New Netherland was under the control of the Dutch. Why this property was given to the Duke of York ties together both economic and political motivations. The bottom line was that the Dutch presence in North America, if left unchecked, could hinder the English attempts to consolidate political control in their North American colonies. Four English ships commanded by Richard Nicolls sailed to New Amsterdam in August of that same year. A letter demanding surrender was sent to Governor Stuyvesant, who delayed as long as he could, but when he realized no help was on the way, he signed a treaty. Nicolls was declared governor, and the city was renamed New York. On June 23, 1664, the Duke of York conveyed a portion of this territory (now the state of New Jersey) to Lord Berkeley and Sir George Carteret.

Philip Carteret, George's son, later became the first English governor of the state. He came on the scene in 1665, planted the seat of government in Elizabethtown and tempted colonists from New England to migrate to New Jersey by offering cheap land. This sat well for some who were enticed to move into this region, but others, those who had earlier purchased their lands from the Indians, began to refuse paying the new proprietors any rent or taxes. The colonies were becoming disturbed by domestic disputes and insurrection a good one hundred years before the Declaration of Independence was drafted.

In 1676, the New Jersey colony was divided into east and west territories. Each territory was given its own governor and proprietary governing body, and this divided the present state along lines running diagonally "from the east side of Little Egg Harbor, straight north, through the country, to the utmost branch of Delaware River." In this alignment, present-day Hunterdon County was part of the west territory. By 1701 and 1702, so many dissensions and disturbances had occurred in both the east and west provinces that the proprietors became wearied of the contentiousness and surrendered their right to govern back to the Crown. Queen Anne accepted the transfer on April 17, 1702. This was the end of proprietary government in New Jersey, and until 1776, this region was under royal rule.

Although Native Americans had relinquished their land rights in Hunterdon County by 1703, they continued to hold a contradictory interpretation of land rights from those they sold the land to. When the Leni-Lenape "sold" land, they thought they would share its use with the buyers. To a European proprietor, a "purchase" meant private and total ownership. This was far more than a cultural misunderstanding: it was the reverberating collision of two opposing world views, and it permeated the brief relationship between Native Americans and Europeans in colonial America and in the Delaware Valley. By the 1750s, European liquor and imported diseases had reduced the Leni-Lenape population to insignificance. While troubles between Native Americans and Europeans faded, the problems among those of European descent who had arrived on different boats did not.

In general, Europeans, many of them squatters, first settled New Jersey from the south along the Delaware Bay shore and from the east starting with areas near the Hudson River and gradually moved north on the Delaware River and west along the Raritan River.

Squatters did not own the land they cleared and farmed, but by the 1750s, they had made their way to regions where the land was good and the owners were absent. Proprietors generally encouraged squatters because their labor in clearing and planting fields enhanced the value of the owner's land. The combination of landless occupants and absent owners shaped the landscape in ways that can still be seen today.

When groups with the common intention of founding a town settled sites, the land would typically be laid out according to an established plan. Villages might be designed with rectangular lots clustered around central common spaces, or greens; long lots might front on water courses to maximize access; and people might concentrate their houses in groups rather than dispense them across the land. But when squatters settled places, the resulting landscape patterns could be far more random. Streets would evolve with peculiar twists and jogs as people moved from place to place, skirting property liens and avoiding obstacles. Early Frenchtown—known at first as Alexandria—was one such unplanned, irregular kind of place.

A RIVER TOWN TAKES SHAPE

In colonial days, the present site of the borough of Frenchtown was a mingling of farmland and untamed wilderness. In 1752, three partners—John Stevens, James Parker and William Alexander—formed a joint stock company and bought around thirty-four thousand acres of West Jersey Society land, including the site of today's Frenchtown Borough and Alexandria Township. At the time, the area we know as Frenchtown was referred to as Calvin's Ferry, named for the operator of the local ferry. Such a river crossing is known to have operated at this location at least as early as 1741. The developing town was to be called Alexandria in honor of William Alexander, though there are references to the region bearing the name of the many ferry operators residing on both sides of the river. At that time, Indian hostilities were well in the past, and many families (most of them of British or German ancestry who had come to New Jersey by way of Pennsylvania) had migrated into the region and squatted on farm sites there.

In 1757, the land's proprietors began efforts to settle the town by laying out streets and building lots, and a year later, they contracted with Samuel Schooley for the construction of a sawmill and dam on the Nishisakawick Creek. Although the 1758 contract does not specify the exact location of the proprietors' mill, local tradition places it on the creek just south of Race Street, where a large stone sawmill, modernized several times, stood until the mid-1970s. Its foundations can still be seen today.

By 1766, few settlers had arrived, so to encourage settlement, the proprietors provided for the establishment of a store. A Philadelphia merchant, Thomas Riche, purchased a lot of land on which he agreed to build a store and dwelling house and keep the store stocked and in operation. This structure stood on the site of today's 10 Bridge Street (which is referred to as the Gem building), near the river, and was operated as a store until the late 1860s. A gristmill on what is now Trenton Avenue was built around the same time. This mill is said to have stood on the site of the Worman Mill (named after its 1868 purchaser), which operated through the 1950s.

Thomas Riche's store and mill were essential elements in the town's development as an agricultural service center. The common practice of bartering was the main form of exchange. Farm produce was traded for imported goods, cloth, imperishable foodstuffs and other trade goods brought from Philadelphia. The gristmill was central to village life, as it processed grain for sale and shipment out to market. Without the store and the gristmill, outlying farmers would not have begun to bring their goods to trade in the settlement that would become Frenchtown. From the 1760s through the '90s, the trade in grain and other farm products grew, with goods being shipped to Philadelphia by Durham boat. In addition to trading with farmers, processing agricultural products and transporting them to market, the hamlet developed a second activity based on timbering and river traffic.

Building a mill to cut wood was a good idea because the Delaware River was already in active use as a lumber chute. Logs bound together and piloted as rafts were transported on the spring and fall currents from upriver forests to markets in Philadelphia and thence to Europe. The community that could haul logs from the river and saw them into lumber and building materials seized an opportunity to add value to this floating timber. Because of the sawmill Schooley built, Alexandria (Calvin's Ferry) became a stopping place for the river men. Those who piloted log rafts and Durham boats found a place to buy and sell cargoes and rafts, hire pilots and, of course, fortify themselves with food and spirits. This went on until timber supplies had become virtually depleted in the mid-nineteenth century.

DURHAM BOATS AND FERRIES

Almost as early as settlers began to locate on the lands along the Delaware, ferries were a necessity. Ferries were operated so early at various points along the river that their actual beginnings are unclear. It is believed that the one operated at the point of the river on which Frenchtown now sits was possibly in existence as early as 1699. The first actual record, however, dates from the year 1741, when it was known as London Ferry. This name was naturally changed from time to time as it passed into the hands of different parties, and in 1764, we find that it was known as Mechlenburgh Ferry. Its later names, in consecutive order, were Erwin, Calvin, Sherod's (or Sherrard's) and Prevost's Ferry. It was finally abandoned with the opening of the bridge in the year 1844.

What were known as Durham boats came into popular use for the carrying of freight on the upper reaches of the river. These boats first came into use in 1727, when the Durham Iron Company was built.

This company owes part of its existence to land dealings orchestrated by William Penn. Around 1676, three Quakers—William Penn, Gawen Lowrie and Nicholas Lucas—bought vast tracts of land in western New Jersey, including large portions of Hunterdon County, and across the river in Pennsylvania. By the turn of the century, Penn was active on both sides of the Delaware. In his capacity as the proprietor of Pennsylvania, he granted important powers to the Free Society of Traders, a group of businessmen based in London, England. The Free Society of Traders was granted tracts of land in Bucks County near present-day Doylestown, Warwick, New Britain, Hilltown and Durham. This group sold the area of land that is now Durham Township to the iron company in 1727. Once the ironworks was up and running, the Durham boats were used to transport the product downriver to Philadelphia.

Durham boats were large, flat-bottomed craft that drew but two or three feet of water when fully loaded and, consequently, could be operated where the stream was quite shallow, allowing for easier shipping of material year-round. The boats were about sixty feet in length, with a thirty- to thirty-five-foot steering oar operated from the rear; hand-operated poles, twelve to eighteen feet long, propelled the boats. In the famous painting *Washington Crossing the Delaware*, he is pictured standing in the front end of a Durham boat, and it was largely this sort of boat that was used to successfully carry the soldiers across to the Jersey shore on the memorable Christmas night in 1776. The last Durham boat to make the river trip from Easton to Philadelphia was in 1860.

The industry based on timber reached its height in 1840 to 1845. Its decline began with the coming of the railroads in the 1850s. In the '30s, it was not uncommon for as many as two thousand log rafts to pass down the river in a single season. An average raft was made up of 65,000 feet of logs. This information allows one to grasp the scope of this early industry. Using just a little multiplication, the number of total logs transported down the river becomes far more than 100 million feet per annum. At Frenchtown, there were several different sawmills located at different points in town. Today, one hears tales of the Wild West where a rough-and-ready crew was always available to work or fight. In the early days of Frenchtown, the lumber industry had brought a similar personality type with it; many of the workers were ready to scrap at the drop of a hat.

In later years, attempts were made to operate steamboats from Lambertville to Easton, but they were soon abandoned. Steamboats as carriers of freight were impractical north of the tidewater at Trenton. The first of these boats to ascend the river between these two points was known as the *Major William Barnett*.

This steamboat first startled the residents of the village by blowing its whistle as it passed Frenchtown on March 13, 1852. A second boat, *The Reindeer*, passed Frenchtown on April 26, 1852. One month later (May 12), a boiler explosion near Point Pleasant ended the career of the *Major William Barnett*. Soon the coming of the railroad ended all attempts at commercial river transportation north of Trenton.

2

BEFORE FRENCHTOWN THERE WAS A REVOLUTION OR TWO

Washington never made use of Calvin's Ferry, but others did. The British general Howe crossed the river using this ferry on Thursday morning, October 2, 1777, after the Battle of the Brandywine. After the Battle of Saratoga, in which a portion of Burgoyne's army was captured by General Gates, the captured British soldiers were marched along a route that took them over the King's Highway, which is the road running north and south through Baptistown (modern-day Route 519). At this point, they turned west toward the river (modern-day Route 12), crossed the Nishisakawick Creek into the village and, proceeding by way of what are now Race and Bridge Streets, moved to the river. There they were ferried across and marched on to an important army post of Revolutionary days located at Carlisle, Pennsylvania. As the Revolution in the colonies wound down, across the Atlantic, things were heating up.

Paul Henri Mallet-Prevost was born in Geneva, Switzerland, in 1756. He was blessed with an excellent education, and at an early age, he entered the banking house of his uncle as a clerk. In 1779, he married Jeanne Elizabeth Patry. Some history books tell us that his bride-to-be had fled from a convent where she was to take the veil so she could be with him.

In 1788, Mallet-Prevost moved with his family to Paris to take up banking connections there. On August 10, 1792, the French Communé, under the leadership of Georges Danton, supplanted the National Assembly. The king and his family were made prisoners, and the King's Swiss Guards were massacred. During the French Revolution of 1792,

Mallet-Prevost, a republican, joined the French army at Alsace as commissary general.

Later, in the midst of the horrible massacres then taking place in Paris, he gathered his family together in the garden of their house and then succeeded in getting them out of Paris. He sent them to Saint André, near the coast, but as France was at war with foreign powers, Mallet-Prevost, being an officer, remained at his post. Not long after securing the safety of his family, Mallet-Prevost was appointed administrator of army convoys and was in Paris when the king was executed on January 21, 1793.

Under the threat of foreign invasion, the French Revolution was entering its last stages, and heads were falling fast. Word came to Mallet-Prevost that his name had been listed among those to be guillotined. It took no time at all for him to decide his immediate escape was necessary. He was pursued, but as the story goes, he daringly rode down a steep cliff on horseback, with bullets flying after him, and succeeded in reaching the coast unharmed.

Mallet-Prevost was finally reunited with his family in Bern, Switzerland, or what we would refer to as the Old City of Bern today. But he was not safe even there and, once more, was obliged to flee. He left his family behind and, via a circuitous route, managed to escape into Germany (remember, much of modern-day Switzerland was occupied by various concerns, including France, at this time). He arrived in Germany with his secretary, Nicolas Louis Toulaine de Fresnoye (Defresnoye), and from there, they moved on to Holland. During his stay in Holland, he was repeatedly seized as a French spy. Eventually he and Fresnoye sailed to England and, in June 1794, on to North America, landing in Philadelphia. When looking for a home and property to own, he visited Alexandria and, delighted with the place, set about buying out Thomas Lowrey. A little more than a year later, he and his family were happily reunited at their new home, where the Nishisakawick Creek flowed into the Delaware River. Fresnoye, who had fled the scene of the French Revolution with Mallet-Prevost, also settled at this point along the banks of the Delaware.

3

A "FRENCH" TOWN IS BORN

Early 1800s

Thomas Lowrey was born in Derryloran, Ireland, on September 3, 1737. He was the son of Sarah Patterson and an unknown father. He and his mother immigrated to New Jersey, and he married Esther Fleming, the daughter of merchant Samuel Fleming (for whom the town of Flemington is named) in 1752. Lowrey became Samuel Fleming's apprentice and later business partner. Early in his career, he became a successful land investor and developer. Around the time of his marriage to Esther Fleming, Lowrey purchased his first piece of land from Mr. Fleming, a 650-foot parcel in what is today Flemington. A store was built on this site, and Lowrey used his profits to purchase more land in the Flemington area. Rather than keeping the land for himself, Lowrey subdivided and sold it to settlers. His business ethics earned Lowrey the nickname "Quicksilver." In 1775, Lowrey became a member of the New Jersey Provincial Congress, and in 1776, he was commissioned as a lieutenant colonel and later colonel of the Third Hunterdon County Militia Regiment.

As evidenced by a deed dated May 20, 1776, Thomas Lowrey purchased a 968-acre tract of land that covered parts of Kingwood and Alexandria Townships where Calvin's Ferry was located from John and Elizabeth Stevens and James and Gertrude Parker. Lowrey continued the proprietors' tradition of absentee ownership (although he did build himself a house, on what is today the bend where Bridge Street becomes Race, and lived here briefly). Lowrey leased parts of this property to tenants rather than sell the lots.

After the American Revolution, Lowrey continued to expand his land holdings and became active in government. Years later, he purchased a 333-

acre tract of land known as Burnt Mills on July 18, 1795, for £2,716. This property was just a few miles north of his Calvin's Ferry acreage. Burnt Mills was renamed Lowreytown. Lowrey's first residence on his new property, the Gibson House, was completed in 1798, but it remained unoccupied by the Lowreys because Mrs. Lowrey disliked it. A second house was built closer to the Delaware River, and this became the Lowrey family's primary residence. The Gibson House later became a hotel. While this second house was under construction, Colonel Lowrey contracted Thomas Elliot to build a gristmill and sawmill in Lowreytown. To buy Burnt Mills and implement all of the visions he had planned for this tract of land, he needed money. To earn money, Lowrey sold his property in and around Calvin's Ferry. The man who bought the property had recently arrived in the New World, Henri Paul Mallet-Prevost, who Lowrey mistakenly thought was a French army officer.

Lowrey died on November 10, 1806, at the age of seventy-two, but many reminders of his legacy have been left behind in both Milford and Frenchtown. Over time, Lowreytown was renamed Millsford. Eventually, the last two letters from "mills" were dropped, and the village settled on the name as it is spelled today.

When he was not renting his Calvin's Ferry property out, Colonel Lowrey tried to sell this riverfront property several times to purchasers he believed would be unable to make the final payments, hence giving ownership back to Lowrey along with the down payments. Mallet-Prevost was a different case. Mallet-Prevost bargained with Colonel Lowrey for the 968 acres with a generous offer of £7,664, and since Lowrey needed funds to construct the mills in Lowreytown, the offer was accepted. At first, Lowrey believed Mallet-Prevost, like the other real estate speculators he had sold the property to, would be unable to make the second and third payments. But, to his utter astonishment, Mallet-Prevost said, "Mr. Lowrey, if you deducts de interest, I pays de second." To this, Lowrey, again in need of the funds, reluctantly consented. Mallet-Prevost then said, "Mr. Lowrey, if you deducts de interest, I pays de third." In Lowrey's sale of the property, the deed bears the date December 4, 1794, and was made to Mallet-Prevost's secretary, Fresnoye. The Calvin's Ferry property was bounded on the south by lands owned by Thomas and Edward Marshall and Ezekiel Rose, on the east by lands owned by Daniel Opdyke and on the west by the Delaware River.

Mallet-Prevost was soon joined in Alexandria by his family and a number of servants and associates. Records indicate that several families with French names such as LaRoche, Femere and Carpentier had arrived with Mallet-Prevost and that slaves were part of his Alexandria household. People began, in the late 1790s, to call the place Frenchtown, after the language so many of its new inhabitants spoke.

One year after the sale of the property, on November 25, 1795, Fresnoye deeded slightly more than sixty-seven acres of this tract to François Dufrene Femere; he in turn deeded it to Lewis D. Carpentier on May 13, 1798. On June 16, 1801, Carpentier passed the title to Andrew Mallet-Prevost. On January 19 of the following year, Fresnoye conveyed slightly more than 825 acres to Andrew Mallet-Prevost so that the entire original purchase of 893 acres now stood in the name of the eldest son of Paul Henri Mallet-Prevost.

When Mallet-Prevost bought the property, a small settlement already existed. Most of the buildings were positioned along what are Bridge and Race Streets today and the area to the south bordering on the Nishisakawick Creek. The only planning for this settlement was a map that delineated streets and lots the absentee owners had drawn. A late nineteenth-century account of this original map states that the streets mapped in 1757 still existed and have been expanded upon. On Mill Street (now Trenton Avenue), a gristmill and sawmill stood, with a headrace connecting the two mills. By 1766, the village also had a general store of sorts on the main street near the river (between what is today 10 and 12 Bridge Street).

To properly settle into their new home, the Mallet-Prevost family had to build new homes. This they did. Three houses were built on the Prevost Homestead lot. The lot extended between the main street (Bridge Street) on the north and the Nishisakawick Creek on the south and between the river and Mill Street to the east. The oldest of these individually interesting buildings is the brick house at 35 Railroad Avenue (now the corner of Front Street and Hawk Street) built by Captain William Conner for Paul Henri. This house, built in 1795, is believed to be the oldest of the three Mallet-Prevost homes and exists pretty much as originally constructed. It is also one of only a few surviving brick-walled pre-twentieth-century dwelling houses. This Mallet-Prevost house has a simple Federal style with a pitched slate roof and a center entry. The building material, brick, was virtually never used in local domestic architecture before the twentieth century. The reason for this is simple: brick was expensive. The closest major brick-making center at the time was in Philadelphia, ergo transported brick was more of a luxury than stone or wood. Brick produced in New York would have been even more difficult to come by. The house Mallet-Prevost had built at the mouth of the Nishisakawick where it flows into the Delaware was for his own occupancy. The house as it stands now is in an excellent state of repair and looks almost as it did when built, except for the addition of a piazza. It is the present home of Frenchtown resident Frederick Lowe.

Paul Henri Mallet-Prevost had this house built in 1795. *Courtesy of David Miller.*

The Mallet-Prevost house as it looks today. Fred Lowe now owns the house. *Courtesy of Brokaw Photography.*

The Mallet-Prevost family built the only other two local houses made of brick during this time. One of these homes is said to be the structure at 8 Kingwood Avenue, though this is slightly outside the Prevost homestead. The other home was built on Front Street. Both houses have been remodeled so much they have lost almost all semblance of their original form. Former mayor James Sherman occupied the house on Front Street in the late 1800s; later, it was the home of the Kerr family, who were prominent members of the business community. Its spacious lawn originally extended down to the river's edge and was famous for its grapes of the well-known Delaware variety. These grapevines originated from cuttings taken from Mallet-Provost's home back in France. Today, if one drew a circle around Frenchtown on a map, without traveling too many miles, you would find many wineries on both sides of the river.

Mallet-Prevost was a tremendously energetic landowner. In addition to the homes, the Mallet-Prevost family also had a hand in the building of a hotel and many other structures on Bridge Street and in the southern part of town. Mallet-Prevost and his sons and associates also encouraged craftsmen and tradesmen to settle in the town, and under his influence, the area grew from a small mill hamlet into a thriving village. Frenchtown's first streets were narrow, bending lanes that connected mills, stores and houses: South Harrison and other streets were later formalized by deeds reserving rights-of-way along these traditional passages. Railroad Avenue/Front Street, Lott Street, Kerr Street and Hawk Street were created by deed as the Mallet-Prevost family sold off its homestead in parcels, reserving rights-of-way to avoid landlocked properties. All of these early streets map Frenchtown's growth and evolution from a single-owner plantation to a town where lots were individually owned.

There was no bridge on Main Street (now Bridge Street) for a good many years. Crossing the river was by means of a hand-poled ferry or flatboat at a point just below the present bridge site. Near the river, on the south side of the street at about the present location of the Bridge Café (the former train depot), was a little watch and clock repair shop operated by Jacob Welch; later it was used as a tailor shop by Daniel Curtis.

The first general supply store in the village (Riche's) was a low story-and-a-half frame structure that was located on what is the southeast corner of Main (Bridge) Street and Front Street today (now occupied by the Gem building). Between the little shop and the sawmill, there were two houses, one other general store and a few little specialty shops.

On the opposite side of Main Street from Riche's store stood a small hotel called the Old Brick Tavern, or Old Brick Hotel. Mallet-Prevost built this riverfront structure in 1805. Next to the Old Brick Tavern was a small general

The Warford House, pictured here in 1903, is now the beautifully restored Frenchtown Inn. *Courtesy of David Miller.*

Gravestones in the Frenchtown Cemetery. *Courtesy of Caroline Scutt.*

store run by W.W. Hedges, who eventually became postmaster and, later on, a partner in the lumber firm of Hedges and Reading. The Old Brick Tavern was later increased in size by an addition to the rear as well as a third story added by Hugh E. Warford. When he lived there, it was renamed the Warford House.

Mallet-Prevost led a provincial life, serving as justice of the peace and as a lay member of the county court. His wife passed away in 1810, and after twenty-five lonely years, Paul Henri died as he had lived, a stranger in a strange land. In his eightieth year, he was laid to rest within sight of the house that had been his home for forty years. Following are the names and records of the sons of Paul Henri Mallet-Prevost and Jeanne Elizabeth Patry, his wife.

Andrew Mallet-Prevost was born in Geneva in 1780. He was fifteen years of age when he arrived in America with his mother and two brothers. For a number of years, he assisted in the management of his father's estate in Alexandria. In 1804, he moved to Philadelphia, where he died in 1850.

Henri Mallet-Prevost was also born in Geneva, in 1783. During his early years, he lived with his parents in Frenchtown, but while still a very young man, he too moved to Philadelphia, where he died in 1843.

Louis Andre Mallet-Prevost was only ten years of age when the family arrived in America. The greater part of his life was spent at Frenchtown. Late in life, upon retiring from business, he moved to Pottstown, Pennsylvania, and died there in 1872.

Below is the inscription that may be read on the tombstone located on the Mallet-Prevost plot, just a few hundred feet from the entrance to the Frenchtown Cemetery:

To the Memory of
Paul Henri Mallet-Prevost
Dec 5th January 1833, AE 79
Jeanne Elizabeth Patry
His wife
Dec in 1810, AE 54
Francis Lewis Mallet-Prevost
His brother
Dec in 1824, AE 60
All natives of Geneva & interred within a few feet of this spot.
This tablet is erected by their surviving descendants in 1837

The Frenchtown we know today took root as a Delaware ferry crossing and grain processing center. The town grew with the arrival of sawmills to accommodate the booming lumber industry and continued to expand as Mallet-Prevost converted his country holdings from a village into a market town.

4

GROWTH IN A MARKET TOWN

1830s to 1860s

In the early 1830s, there was no Harrison Street. In fact, there was nothing but the beginning of a lane at what is now Bridge and Harrison. This lane followed the present course of the street up to Second and then turned east and ended at about the present site of the town hall.

On the southeast corner of this alley stood a little old frame farmhouse that was, for forty years, the home of Louis LaRoche, who afterward built the American Hotel (later known as the Temperance House). Hann & Williams later used the old farmhouse as an office until both it and their spoke mill were destroyed by the 1878 fire.

In 1836, Hugh Capner came from Flemington, bought a considerable strip of land (181.68 acres) north of Main Street from Mallet-Prevost and opened Harrison Street up to its present intersection with Fifth Street. He also laid out the cross streets from Milford Road to the river. Beyond the point of Fifth Street was the Capner farm. The barn associated with this farmhouse was located at the present junction of Sixth and Harrison Streets. The line fence that blocked the end of Harrison Street at Fifth was crossed by means of a short flight of steps leading to the top of the fence and down on the other side. There was not much growth beyond Fifth Street until Samuel B. Hudnit bought a lot in 1848 and continued to build.

BUILDING BRIDGES—OR A BRIDGE

As commerce and travel throughout the region grew, the ferries alone could not handle the traffic crossing the Delaware. Over time, these were phased out as the towns vied with one another to build bridges. In 1841, a charter was granted for the construction of the first bridge across the Delaware at Frenchtown—the Uhlerstown-Frenchtown Bridge. The Milford Bridge was completed slightly earlier than the one at Frenchtown. Whether a real rivalry was in the works between the two towns or it was just one of the Milford citizens making fun of his southern neighbors, a particular remark was jotted down: "Frenchtown had better build a poorhouse."

Lewis M. Prevost, John Rodenbaugh, Hugh Capner and others pushed the charter project through to a successful conclusion. By 1843, the structure was partially finished, allowing foot traffic over the bridge, and by 1844, construction of the covered wooden structure was completed. This bridge would last until the freshet of 1903.

FRENCHTOWN'S FIRST HOUSES OF WORSHIP

The first Methodist church to be built in Frenchtown was put together in a hurry. In 1843, a small group of Methodists had resolved to build a church, and a board of trustees was elected. They purchased land from Hugh Capner for $100, and construction began. Building operations started in the fall of 1844, and during 1845, strenuous efforts were made to finish the building. This didn't come to pass, so rough boards were used as pews and a temporary altar was built so that the building was operational for preaching in 1845. The building was not completed until the following year and was dedicated on December 17, 1846. In 1895, during the pastorate of the Reverend Elkanah H. Conklin, the last dollar of mortgage indebtedness was paid off, and at impressive Sunday morning services, the $1,500 mortgage was burned after having hung over the church for about twenty-five years. Frenchtown United Methodist Church, located at 16 Third Street, continues to welcome worshipers today.

The Presbyterian church grew out of services held in the wheelwright shop at the northwest corner of the alley between Second and Third Streets on Harrison. The families of Joseph Kugler, Philip G. Reading and Joseph Case gathered here with their neighbors for services in the early 1840s. The

A sketch of the Frenchtown Methodist Church on Third Street. *Courtesy of Rick Epstein, from the Gloria Sipes Paleveda Collection.*

First Presbyterian Church edifice was erected in 1845 on the present site of the town hall on Second Street.

The present church on Fourth Street was built in 1854. The chapel was later erected to the east of the main building and dedicated as a memorial to the first wife of the Reverend W.H. Filson, who was the pastor at that time. The pipe organ installed in the church on April 4, 1901, was the first in Frenchtown; the Methodist organ was put in during the pastorate of the Reverend Charles W. Wright, 1917–18.

As early as 1839 there had been occasional visitations by Baptist preachers, and a little band had come to hope someday to be able to organize a Baptist church in the village. In 1859, the Reverend J.G. Penny was appointed as a missionary to Belvidere and Frenchtown. For a time, the little congregation

The Frenchtown skyline in the 1950s looking north past the National Hotel toward the churches on Second, Third and Fourth Streets. *From* Frenchtown Centennial, 1867–1967.

had use of the Methodist property and, later, that of the Christian church on Kingwood Avenue. The Baptist congregation erected a permanent home on Second Street that was dedicated on Christmas Day 1861. Unfortunately, this structure is no longer in use by the congregation for which it was built.

While there was a time when most residents belonged to one of these three congregations or to the Christian church built on Kingwood Avenue in 1846, today, Frenchtown reflects the decline in church membership seen throughout the United States.

FRENCHTOWN'S POSTAL SYSTEM

Mail delivery in the early days of the colonies was slow, difficult and more or less uncertain. At first, the mail was carried on horseback and then by stage as the roads were improved and the number of roads increased. In 1729, mail between the cities of New York and Philadelphia passed each way once a week in summer and once a fortnight or less in winter, depending, of course, on weather conditions. Little or no improvement was shown up to 1754, but by 1764, mail was being carried three times weekly between these points. The mail was placed in canvas sacks and required twenty-four hours for a one-way, with a change of horses every twenty miles or so along the route. In 1791, there were just six post offices in the state.

The post office in Frenchtown dates from 1839, when the mail was carried on horseback from Trenton by the way of Stockton and Kingwood. At that time, Route 29, which today parallels the river between Trenton and Frenchtown, was nonexistent. After arriving in Frenchtown, the mailman crossed the Delaware on a bateau to continue his delivery route to Erwinna, Pennsylvania. The cost of sending a letter varied from six and a quarter cents to twenty-five cents.

The local post office in Frenchtown was first in the store of Allen and Everts, with one of the partners acting as the first postmaster. This was the store on the corner of Bridge Street and Trenton Avenue later known as Louis M. Prevost's Big Gun store. In later years, the post office moved to various locations on Bridge Street, usually in the home or business of the postmaster. However, on March 12, 1932, the post office was moved to a building at 16 Trenton Avenue and has remained at the site ever since.

In 1960–61, the old post office building was torn down, and a new brick building was erected on the site. It was dedicated in July 1961 when United States senator Harrison Williams presented an American flag that had flown over the Capitol in Washington, D.C., to Postmaster Paul R. Cronce.

The postmaster in his car. The steering mechanism in this old runabout was a handle instead of a wheel. *Courtesy of David Miller.*

Cronce accepted the flag on behalf of the postal employees and the citizens of Frenchtown.

The business of the Frenchtown Post Office has increased dramatically, though the population of the town itself has remained relatively small since the opening of the office on Trenton Avenue. One big reason for the increase in postings came from the growth in the chicken hatchery business. It has been estimated that over 3.5 million chicks were shipped through the Frenchtown Post Office in 1923, and the industry had not yet reached its peak. And while it is a far cry from mail on horseback at six and a quarter cents per letter to the current postage rate, it is always fun to see what the postman drops in the mailbox.

A SNAPSHOT OF FRENCHTOWN'S BUSINESS COMMUNITY IN THE 1800S

In the 1830s, Louis M. Prevost and his son operated the old frame store at the corner of Bridge Street and Trenton Avenue as the Big Gun. Later, Andrew Roberson operated it under the same name. A former resident remarked, "At last the 'Big Gun' was overcharged and it 'busted,' and no doubt some of the fragments can still be found around Frenchtown." In 1876, Roberson's assignees sold out to Philip G. Reading and his sons, James and Charles, who opened the store for business in the spring of 1877.

The year 1836 not only brought the migration of Hunterdon County residents like Hugh Capner, but others, such as Robert L. Williams from New York State, also arrived in Frenchtown. Williams soon began the building of improved fan mills for cleaning grain, the first ever made in the county. He occupied an old shop near the dwelling once belonging to the tannery of Mathias Pickel. Williams also made grain-cradles with bent fingers. He began cultivating broomcorn, which he made into—wait for it—brooms.

In 1845, Philip G. Reading and W.W. Hedges began a partnership to create a lumber business where the spoke factory stood between Second and Third Streets. A year or two later, they built a steam sawmill for making siding. In 1858, Mr. Reading introduced the turning of axe-handles and wagon-spokes. In 1859, Mr. Kugler entered into partnership with Mr. Reading in the spoke and handle factory and carried on the business until 1869, when the factory burned. Kugler & Fargo (the father of Clarence Fargo) rebuilt it, and the same firm continued into the late 1880s.

In 1846, Jesse Sinclair moved to Frenchtown and carried on the mason trade. He built many, if not all, the stone houses in Frenchtown in this period. In 1851, Augustus Godly built the distillery just below the mouth of Little Nishisakawick, where he carried on for a year or two and failed. The aptly named Samuel Drinkhouse of Easton, Pennsylvania, purchased the property and carried on the distillery business for many years; the buildings used for this trade were burned in 1874. Afterward, a lime-burning business—run by Philip Lair, Joseph Kugler and others—existed there for several years.

On the corner now occupied by the three-story brick Hummer Building (29–39 Bridge Street) and prior to the erection of a two-and-a-half-story frame building earlier on this site, Thomas Pittinger, father of H.H. (Okey) Pittinger, had a blacksmith shop and frame dwelling there. Later, he moved his blacksmith shop to the opposite side of Bridge Street, where a brick building now stands. This is where Okey kept store for so many years and sold "most everything from a needle to a locomotive," according to Frenchtown business owner and historian Clarence Fargo. The first drugstore in the village later occupied part of the old Pittinger house and was owned by John Hull. Pittinger built a home (28 Bridge Street) next to his shop, and the building stands directly opposite the mouth of Harrison Street. The house

Pittinger's place of business (32 Bridge Street) and his home (28 Bridge Street) are both still in use today. *Courtesy of Brokaw Photography.*

was built in 1869 and is currently occupied on the first floor by The Book Garden. In later years, Okey moved to the back of the brick store, on South Harrison Street, where he had erected a new dwelling.

The A&P (Atlantic and Pacific Tea Company) occupied space opposite the Union National Bank, which sat on the northwest corner of Bridge and Harrison Streets. Before the A&P operated in this space, it had been occupied by a smaller building in which Lewis M. Prevost had his office as justice of the peace. In 1838, the first Sunday school in Frenchtown, run by a governess employed by the Prevost family, sat on the site. Later, the present-day building was erected, and at first, its entrance was high up in the air, as was the style, with a flight of five or six steps leading to it. In this building, Oliver Worman ran a general store. Afterward, Worman built the large three-story brick store a few lots to the west that is now known as the Gem building (10 Bridge Street) and was, for a time, occupied by Wilmot Milbury. Worman also had a stone residence next to the store built. This house (12 Bridge Street) was once occupied by Eliza Apgar and is referred to as the Apgar House, or the Worman-Apgar House. Worman moved to the new site (Gem building) in 1869.

The Apgar House (12 Bridge Street) is still as pleasant a sight to behold today as it was when built back in 1869. *Courtesy of Brokaw Photography.*

As mentioned earlier, H.H. Pittinger built his house just a few lots down from the Apgar House in 1869. Both homes were built in an Italianate style (a very popular design in the United States between 1840 and 1885). The designers and builders of these homes are not known, but it is likely they were not locally trained. While these homes were being built at the same time as other Italianate style homes in the Slater & Hudnit property, they are completely different from the uptown houses in both looks and construction. The Apgar House features much more of the Italianate personality—such as the symmetrical rectangular shape, tall appearance, square cupola, porches topped with balconies and side bay windows—than the Pittinger house, but both structures make use of wide eaves with brackets and cornices and heavy double doors on the inside. The Apgar House has always been regarded as the most elegant domestic building in Frenchtown. The H.H. Pittinger House, like the Apgar House, is a very distinctive house for Frenchtown.

A bank, a good bank, is the heart of any business community, pumping the financial lifeblood through the veins of its economic structure. In Frenchtown, that lifeblood was originally delivered by the Union Bank of Frenchtown. In 1856, the Union Bank was incorporated as a state bank, with Harry Lott as the first president and Newberry Williams as cashier. In 1865, the state charter was surrendered, and the bank then became a national bank, named the Union National Bank.

The first banking house was located on Second Street, near the southeast corner of Harrison Street. It was a two-and-a-half-story frame structure with large pillars in front. This building was destroyed in the fire of 1878. The bank reopened promptly for business in the residence on the northeast corner of Second and Harrison Streets.

The bank remained at this location until its new home was built on Bridge Street. The new bank was a redbrick building and was completed before the year was out. A fine new front, with a modern vault and bank fittings, was an improvement made in 1923 at a total cost of about $40,000. A safe deposit department was added at the same time.

The Union National Bank of Frenchtown printed national currency worth $1,648,310 starting when it opened as a national entity in 1865 and stopped printing money in 1935. This is a considerably long operation period for a national bank. During its life, the Union National Bank issued twenty-one different types and denominations of national currency. A $20 1929 bank note issued by the bank is now worth about $1,000.

During the life of the bank, two attempts at robbery were reported. A gang of five or six men made the first attempt shortly after midnight on

September 18, 1873. At this time, the old banking house on Second Street had living rooms for the cashier's family on the first floor at the rear of the bank and bedrooms on the second floor. During the robbery attempt, members of the gang gained entrance to the building, proceeded to the door of the bedroom of the cashier, William S. Stover, and his wife and attempted to force the bedroom door, no doubt with the intention of compelling Mr. Stover to open the bank safe.

The husband and wife team quickly responded. Mr. Stover braced himself against the door to hold them out while Mrs. Stover raised a window and called out, "Murder!" A pistol shot was fired from the street, undoubtedly as a signal to the gang members inside the bank, who then made a quick getaway without having gained anything from their attempt. They did manage to steal two horses and a wagon from elsewhere in town and used them to escape.

The second attempt, also gaining the robbers nothing, was made on the night of December 7, 1888, when an entrance was forced at the rear of the new bank building on Bridge Street. Attempts to jimmy the vault failed.

The Union National Bank had its main door at 21 Bridge Street until 1958. This is when the historic Victorian home, built in 1882 for Senator William H. Martin, was torn down to accommodate a drive-through window and direct access to Harrison Street for the bank. In more recent times, as banks throughout the country have undergone a high degree of merging or outright takeover, there has been a changing of the guard at the Frenchtown Bank. The Union National became the First Federal, then the First Union, then the Hudson United and then T.D. North; now, at this writing, a branch of T.D. Bank operates out of this location.

In addition to the bank, in the mid-1860s, attempts were made to begin a building and loan organization. These organizations were extremely important to many citizens in financing the building and/or purchase of a home. The first attempt along these lines was started in Frenchtown on January 15, 1866. This building and loan organization ran for thirteen years. Another Frenchtown building and loan association was organized in 1922 with Chester A. Niece as president. Niece was born (February 24, 1888) and raised in Frenchtown. He began his business career with a portable sawmill and, in 1912, with his father, Israel Niece, opened a retail lumberyard in Frenchtown. In 1920, he bought out Lambert and Kerr (coal and feed dealers) and opened the C.A. Niece Company, subsequently adding a lumberyard. For many years, Niece, Harry D. Blair Sr. and Harry D. Blair Jr. ran the company. This operation evolved into a building supply firm in

Left: The Union National Bank on Bridge Street. *Courtesy of Caroline Scutt.*

Below: The Martin residence, which in 1903 graced the corner of Bridge and Harrison, was torn down and replaced by a bank drive-through and a parking lot. *Courtesy of David Miller.*

the 1950s when Niece sold to Harry Blair Sr. and is run as Niece Lumber out of Lambertville today. Niece was also mayor of Frenchtown in 1918–19 and 1929–30 and served on the Frenchtown School Board for twenty-five years.

Hotels and Inns

By the mid-1800s there were three operating hotels in Frenchtown. The National was called the Upper Hotel. The Lower Hotel, like the National, still exists today. It is known as the Frenchtown Inn. Lewis F. LaRoche built the third structure, the Middle Hotel, in the early 1840s, near what is now the corner of Bridge and Harrison Streets. LaRoche was the son of Zachariah LaRoche, who came to this section of Hunterdon County with Paul Henri Mallet-Prevost in the late 1700s. The Middle Hotel was the American Hotel; it was later known as the Temperance House. The Middle Hotel was destroyed in the 1878 fire.

Before any of these three hotels were on the scene a tavern near the river was a favorite watering hole and stopover place for those traveling between New York and Philadelphia. Paul Henri Mallet-Prevost built the tavern in 1805. In 1806, John Britton began the construction of what would become known at the Rail Road House. This structure was built up and over the Mallet-Prevost tavern and included portions of the original structure that were used as a shop to cure and finish leather. At first, this new hotel was called the Old Brick Tavern and is so named in deeds. On April 31, 1837, William Case bought acreage from Lewis Prevost, and in the deed, the Old Brick Tavern is referred to as the "tavern" lot.

In anticipation of the Phillipsburg-to-Trenton rail line, in 1838, the Old Brick Tavern was renamed the Rail Road House. Much of the hotel as we know it today was completed at this time, but though the hotel was named the Rail Road House, it wasn't until 1853 that the first train came over the tracks as far as Frenchtown. The original name of the completed railroad was the Belvidere and Delaware. You can still see the mile markers enumerating the distance between the destinations along the route. With the coming of the railroad and the thriving local mills and river traffic, the town grew, and the Rail Road House prospered. The path taken by the railroad between Frenchtown and Trenton still exists but has been converted into a Rails-to-Trails and is part of the Delaware and Raritan Canal State Park.

The Frenchtown Inn, where patrons can enjoy an outdoor table with a view of the river, 2010. *Courtesy of Brokaw Photography.*

The Frenchtown Train Station (depot), 1903. The Frenchtown Inn is on the same side of the street as the cameraman (to the left), facing the train depot. *Courtesy of David Miller.*

The Rail Road House was purchased by a member of the Warford family in 1890 and become known as the Warford House. The inn remained in that family's possession until 1946. It continued to operate as a tavern and boardinghouse under various owners throughout the years. In 1985, a renovation project was started, and today, the building is known as the Frenchtown Inn. Much of the renovation efforts focused on the dining rooms and bar areas on the first floor. The results of these labors helped turn the Frenchtown Inn into a dining establishment often being rated as one of the top places to eat in the state. Thanks in part to its executive chef and owner, Andrew Tomko—who, with his wife, Colleen, purchased the inn in 1996—the inn upholds and expands on its reputation for fine cuisine.

Since the 1850s (over a century and a half ago), one of the first signs you have arrived in Frenchtown, if traveling from the east or south, has been the National Hotel, or Upper Hotel. The building stands at the town's entrance from both these directions, at the intersection of State Route 12 and County Route 513. In 1850, Robert L. Williams built the National, and it has been owned and/or operated by various owners, including William Apgar in the late 1880s. Samuel Powers had built a blacksmith shop on that spot in 1833 and mounted a sign advertising rooms for rent in a road-front structure while he did his work in the stable behind. The Sign of the Buck served as a brothel and stagecoach stop until 1850, when Williams replaced it with the current structure, naming it the National Hotel. Inspired by the arrival of the Belvidere and Delaware Railroad and emergent industrial development along the river, the National was one of the three accommodations constructed to court the flourishing business in town. In the 1890s, additions were made to the National, which also continued to serve as blacksmith shop, stable, saloon, billiard parlor and restaurant. Hotel legend boasts of such illustrious guests as Annie Oakley and Buffalo Bill Cody in the late 1800s.

A succession of owners coaxed the proud old inn through good times and bad in the twentieth century. In the 1970s, the Broadway theater actress and cabaret performer Claiborne Cary visited the National when she wasn't, like her older sister, Cloris Leachman, appearing on television. Claiborne and her friends Mary Tyler Moore and Valerie Harper frequently took the limo out from the city for cabaret nights in Frenchtown. On Saturday nights, the story goes, Claiborne would appear dressed in a full-length evening gown to play the piano.

If you desire to learn more about the National, ask Pete or Marie D'Costa, whose affair with the building began in 2009. The National had stood padlocked and shuttered for almost three years, a victim of imperfect management in difficult economic circumstances. For visitors to Frenchtown, the sheets of plywood that covered the windows painted a bleak picture during these times. Luckily for Frenchtown, Pete and Marie made an offer. They did not really expect to be in contention since there were bids from two competing investment groups, but the realtor called in June 2009. They closed on the sale in July, and to the relief of the townspeople of Frenchtown, the plywood came off as soon as the renovations were underway. The National reopened in November 2009.

In this section, we listed the three hotels that were part of the Frenchtown landscape in the mid-1880s. As described, the National and the Frenchtown Inn are still in operation, but in addition to these establishments, there have always been other venues in which one could spend a night or two. Today, these establishments are called bed-and-breakfast inns. They tend to dot the landscape in some of the older, more rustic homes and buildings. For example, today in Frenchtown, if one is looking for a weekend getaway, you would be a stone's throw from the heart of the business district at the Widow McCrea House. This is a charming Victorian house built in 1878 on Kingwood Avenue just a few blocks southeast of the Nishisakawick Creek.

Across the river in Erwinna, one can find an older bed-and-breakfast, the Golden Pheasant Inn. The land on which this inn is located was part of the

The National Hotel (often referred to as the Upper Hotel) in 1908. *Courtesy of David Miller.*

London company (the Free Society of Traders) land grant and became part of Arthur Erwin's property in 1769. Arthur Erwin is best known for his role in assisting Washington with the crossing of the Delaware River on Christmas night in 1776. In 1811, Joseph Haney acquired a portion of this land for £550 and applied for a tavern license. The construction of a tavern in this location, like those in Frenchtown, grew out of area farmers' need for a place to eat or sleep as they traveled River Road (now identified as Route 32) with their grain. In 1786, River Road had been extended from Lumberville north through Erwinna, where London Ferry (Calvin's Ferry) was located, and on to the Durham furnace near Kintnersville. The Durham furnace was the manufacturing hub for different iron goods. London Ferry was, of course, the crossing point to Frenchtown, New Jersey, and markets north.

SCHOOL DAYS

In the early 1800s, it was common to try to situate a schoolhouse as centrally as possible for the convenience of the greatest number. Consequently, at the beginning of the school record, we find reference to two schoolhouses. One was on Baptistown Road (Kingwood Avenue, also known as Route 12) just past the lane leading in to the Luther Force farmhouse. This school, we are told, did not last long. Another school was located in the other end of town. This school was located in the Hollow, or Shuster's Hollow, just past what is Twelfth Street today, off Milford Road. This structure was built in 1852. An older school was built in the 1840s on land owned by Isaac Johnson. This school was located on Second Street; however, Johnson's business failing led to the property's foreclosure. The citizens of the town then did something that was not unusual at the time: they moved the building and placed it on a piece of land owned by Philip G. Reading.

At the intersection of Kingwood Avenue and what is known as Ridge Road today, a small single-room stone schoolhouse was erected for the children living east and south of the creeks. At the time the building was constructed, the section of the present borough lying along Kingwood Avenue was a part of Kingwood Township and known as either Hensburg or Hentown. This section was afterward added to the borough of Frenchtown. Around the same time, there was also a private school conducted for a time by a Miss Smith in the old Presbyterian church building on Second Street, now the town hall site.

In 1858, Hugh Capner donated a piece of land along Everittstown Road for use in the creation of a new school building. The structure was built along the ridgeline overlooking the town. When construction was completed, it sat between Everittstown Road and what was then Reading Avenue. Reading Avenue no longer exists. Today, Cedar Avenue connects Everittstown Road with the houses built along the ridgeline. Those attending school in the single-room stone house were moved to the new framed structure. The new school became known as Hillside Academy. Hillside Academy was later enlarged so that four large, light-filled schoolrooms were in the building.

In 1900, the old Hillside Academy was sold and removed, and a modern structure was erected, with local carpenter John Lancaster as the contractor. The cost of this schoolhouse was $11,000. Two years of high school courses were added to the curriculum, with the junior and senior years being completed by commuting the students by train to the Lambertville High School.

It is not known what caused this fine building to catch fire, but it burned to the ground on the morning of March 20, 1923. The fire was discovered about 7:00 a.m., and in little more than an hour, the structure was only a memory. The immense chimney and warped, twisted fire escapes stood for a while as reminders of the past. Today, there are only homes standing along Cedar Avenue, most with a fine view of historic Frenchtown below.

Hillside Academy was one of Frenchtown's first schools. *Courtesy of Rick Epstein, from the Gloria Sipes Paleveda Collection.*

At this point, we shall briefly mention the schoolhouse built in Shuster's Hollow in 1852. This operation was in existence until 1875. Over its lifetime, the school had thirty-seven different teachers; a number of them later became lawyers, doctors, ministers, editors and so on. The Honorable John C. Besson (an uncle of U.S. District Attorney Harlan Besson) taught in this school in 1856. He later moved to Hoboken and was elected as a member of the General Assembly for 1885–86. The Honorable George O. Vanderbilt taught in 1864 and was elected to the General Assembly in 1873 and again in 1874, in which year he was also chosen Speaker of the House. He was also elected as a state senator in 1864. The Reverend Daniel M. Matthews, for many years a pillar in the Frenchtown Methodist Church, taught in 1861–62. Simeon R. Opdycke taught in 1863, and afterward, he taught at Hillside Academy. Ross Slack, who for a short time published the *Frenchtown Enterprise*, taught in 1870.

We return now to the borough schools and the problem facing its citizens and the school board after the fire destroyed Hillside Academy. For three years, public school sessions were conducted in the chapel of the Presbyterian church, the basements of the two other churches and in the town hall. Finally in 1925, an agreeable solution to the problem was reached. A plot of ground on Harrison Street above Eighth Street, which extended through to Milford Road, was chosen as the site of the new school and purchased. A modern (for the times) two-story building of brick and stone was erected at a cost of $136,000. The new school opened on September 2, 1926, with all elementary and middles school grades and a complete four-year high school. It was built with twelve spacious, light-filled, well-ventilated schoolrooms, including a gymnasium and auditorium. It was, without doubt, a school building that any community of this size might be justly proud to possess. Even today, it stands the test of time when compared with more modern schools in other towns and cities. Professor Leigh M. Lott was brought in as the first supervising principal and ably assisted by a full corps of efficient teachers. Professor Bertram M. Light succeeded Professor Lott in 1931, the latter having accepted a place as supervising principal at Salem, New Jersey.

Students arrived at the Frenchtown School from near and far, some commuting by train and others by school buses. In 1932, Clarence Fargo reported the enrollment of students, from town and elsewhere, to be about 425 boys and girls. This included those attending high school. Today, only kindergarten through eighth-grade students attend this school, with an enrollment of 136. If one compares this number with the enrollment reported for the Hillside Academy in 1893 (93 pupils) and the population density of the town from the 1880s until 2010, only minor changes in the

When first built, the Frenchtown School on Harrison Street included grades K–12. Today, the school is called the Edith Ort Thomas Elementary School. The older students now attend class at Delaware Valley High School. *Courtesy of Caroline Scutt.*

overall population is observed. Fargo also reported the value of the school, fully equipped, to be close to $165,000. Today, the school property alone is worth millions of dollars.

THE CIVIL WAR

Life in the 1860s was not, of course, the swiftly rushing scene in which we live today. There was no Internet; there weren't even telephones or radios. In Civil War days, there was not even a telegraph office in Frenchtown (this didn't arrive until May 1864), and newspapers were few, slow and far between. With the firing at Fort Sumter in 1861, which began the bloody strife that set brother against brother and lasted for four long years, everyone was hungry for news and filled with anxiety. At this time, a respected citizen named Arthur W. Lundy, who operated a small watch repair shop, would frequently perch himself on a box or other elevation on the porch of the store next to his little shop and read aloud to the assemblage the latest news and casualty list from whichever newspapers were available.

As in all other wars, the conflict was hoped to be short, and so the national government steadfastly refused to accept more than a limited number of volunteers. At the beginning of the conflict (April 1861), the total number of men in uniform in the army was around 16,000. Shortly after the shelling of Fort Sumter, the federal government asked for 75,000 ninety-day volunteers to help put down the insurrection. Governor Olden of New Jersey had offered to furnish additional regiments, but the offer was repeatedly declined. Peace was expected in a few short months. But many disasters befell the Federal armies, and the dream of a short war passed. President Lincoln eventually had to issue a call for 500,000 men for a three-year enlistment or for the duration of the war.

In response to this call, a public meeting was held in Frenchtown on July 22, 1862. William H. Slater, then one of the local merchants, spoke at the meeting, stating that he had already enlisted in the service of his country and called on others to come forward and do likewise. Many did so, and Slater was chosen as captain of Company G, a unit of the Flemington-based Fifteenth New Jersey Volunteers regiment. He received his commission as captain on August 15, 1862. Second in command of this Flemington-based unit was First Lieutenant Suydam Crater, followed by Second Lieutenant John D. Trimmer. Before the recruits started for the scene of hostilities, they practiced their drills on a vacant lot along the railroad between Fourth and Fifth Streets. At that time, the only nearby houses were those on Harrison Street.

Captain Slater led the regiment off to war on August 29, 1862. There were stirring scenes at the train depot when the soldiers bid their sweethearts, wives, relatives and friends a tearful farewell as they departed for camp and the battlefield. Some would never return, as dictated by the fortunes of war. The Fifteenth New Jersey Volunteers fought in a long list of engagements from December 13, 1862, at the first battle of Fredericksburg to Lee's surrender at Appomattox, Virginia, on April 9, 1865. With the Union preserved as the fruits of the long and bloody struggle, the soldiers returned home to the pursuits of everyday life. Unfortunately for Captain Slater, his services were cut short. At the first Battle of Fredericksburg, he was so badly wounded that his right limb had to be amputated.

Captain Slater survived and, after the war, moved with his family to Washington, D.C., to assume a role in the Commissary Department.

Left: The traditional Memorial Day gun salute on the bridge. *Courtesy of Brokaw Photography.*

Below: The Frenchtown Memorial Day Parade. *Courtesy of Brokaw Photography.*

His new home was, like that of the president of the United States, on Pennsylvania Avenue. He died in 1900, and his remains are buried in the Frenchtown Cemetery.

In the words of Clarence Fargo:

> *It seems but a yesterday when, on Memorial Day, we would see these veterans of the Civil War in their uniforms of blue, and wearing black slouch hats decorated with the gold cord and the GAR insignia; as with firm tread they marched at the head of the procession, with Old Glory flung to the breeze and carried before them as they proceeded to the silent city, there to render homage to the memory of their departed comrades and, having decorated the graves with flowers carried by the school children, firing a salute, and listening to a prayer and to the speeches of the day, now departing for their homes, to return again with rapidly thinning ranks on next Memorial Day.*

With the passing of the years came the day when the last few aged veterans, too infirm to make the customary pilgrimage on foot, were conveyed in the parade by automobile to the cemetery so they could once again memorialize the honored dead. During the Memorial Day celebrations of our time, the salute is given to the fallen heroes from the bridge as a wreath is dropped into the river from a flyby overhead. The last Frenchtown veterans of the Civil War and World War I have gone to join the innumerable throng, while the numbers remaining from the actions overseas in World War II, the Korean conflict and the Vietnam War are dwindling. A younger generation now occupies the stage of life as new conflicts continuously emerge, and this is why we still observe Memorial Day—to pay homage to the veterans, old and new, of the American Legion.

5

POST–CIVIL WAR FLOURISHING

1860s to 1900

Images we know today from movies and television shows of towns out in the Wild West are really illustrations of all towns in the 1800s. For many years, Frenchtown had no streetlights, and if one had occasion to be out on a dark night, it was best to carry a lantern to avoid mishaps. Sidewalks, if there were any at all, were mostly made of hemlock boards nailed down to stringers, and it was always possible a board would come loose at one end, fly up and bring about a loss of dignity, if not something worse. The public streets were ankle-deep in dust or sticky mud, and the only street cleaners were the ladies who wore the prevailing fashion of the day, the trailing skirt.

Over time, streetlamps were placed at intersections along Harrison and Bridge Streets, with a few elsewhere, and a man was employed to tend them at the generous pay of nine dollars monthly. Excepting in periods of full moon, when the lamps were not lit, the lamplighter visited each lamp every morning to extinguish the lights and fill and clean the lamps. To do this, he needed to carry a short ladder and a five-gallon can with him both in the evening to light the lamps and in the morning to clean them. Needless to say, he earned his money.

In the post–Civil War days, Frenchtown was somewhat quiet, until Samuel B. Hudnit and Gabriel Slater came on the scene. These men, who were trade partners, operated a hardware store at what later became the Eddy location and also employed a number of hands to manufacture wagons, sleighs and harnesses.

Slater & Hudnit initiated a new land development scheme that had the potential to double Frenchtown's size. The hardware merchants bought the undeveloped north portion of Hugh Capner's tract in 1866, laid out the streets between Fifth and Twelfth Streets and immediately started development. At the time, Harrison Street extended only to Fifth, with a farm to the north of Fifth Street. George Eddy's residence was that farmhouse. Through Slater & Hudnit's efforts, Frenchtown has the distinction of being one of the only (or perhaps *the* only) speculator towns built in Hunterdon County. This is clearly demonstrated by the similarity of houses built in the borough during the last half of the nineteenth century. The first houses built in this section were on the southeast corner of Fifth and Harrison. After this, a number of other homes on the north side of upper Fifth Street were built.

The purchased property was farmed for a year before the streets were laid out and building lots offered for sale. At first, sales were slow, but with a rumor spreading that the Pennsylvania Railroad was going to move its shops to Frenchtown, and later that another large factory was going to be located in the upper end of the development, the boom was on. Sales of sites became brisk and building commenced. Unfortunately for those investing in Frenchtown real estate, the law of economics—that after each boom there shall come a bust—set in. Clouds began to appear on the economic horizon in the early 1870s, followed by the panic of 1873. Frenchtown had been overbuilt, and the next step was inevitable. People could not meet the payments on their obligations and lost what they had put into their properties, business concerns went into bankruptcy and notes in the bank were left unpaid.

While a great deal of overdevelopment had occurred before the panic of 1873, these structures did help lay the groundwork for the borough since the buildings that were completed before the panic did eventually become useful. In other words, the place later grew into the overexpansion that had taken place in the post–Civil War days.

Under an act of the New Jersey legislature, Frenchtown was incorporated as a borough on April 4, 1867. Until this date, the town was part of the township of Alexandria. The first meeting under this charter was held on the second Monday of April in the same year.

Samuel B. Hudnit was instrumental in creating the sentiment resulting in the incorporation of Frenchtown as a borough, and he was elected its first mayor that same year. The mayoral term was one year, and Hudnit was elected two more times in nonconsecutive years, once in 1870 and again in 1872. Several others have held nonconsecutive terms as Hudnit did. The first common council for the borough was composed of I.W. Carmichael, Henry Lott, Philip G. Reading, J.H. Black, Oliver Worman and Moses K. Everitt. The town clerk was James Dilts.

Hudnit built and lived in the three-story brick house on the northeast corner of Fourth and Harrison Streets, where he died suddenly on February 11, 1873, at the comparatively young age of fifty-one. Today, Warren Cooper is the fifty-first elected mayor of Frenchtown Borough.

An interesting section of the original charter deals with the matter of loans and debt, and although this regulation has long since been superseded by later acts, the restriction placed on the authorities then is mentioned here as a matter of interest. This section reads: "…shall not be a greater sum than one thousand dollars raised by loan in any one year, and that the said Borough shall not owe over two thousand dollars at one time." Obviously, times have changed.

The charter placed the power to grant license for the sale of intoxicating liquors in the hands of the common council, and such licenses were permitted by a majority vote. Later, and until the passing of the Eighteenth Amendment, the issuing of licenses was taken from the local councils by an act of the legislature and placed in the hands of the judge of the county court. In those days, when the council granted licenses, the sentiment was more or less evenly divided, and there was more than one, as Fargo wrote, "pretty fight," political and otherwise, over the subject of liquor sales. Even preachers did not always refrain from mentioning names directly from the pulpit.

On January 4, 1878, the Frenchtown Temperance Association was organized, with Reverend James H. Runyan, the Methodist preacher, as president. The purpose of this temperance association was, simply put, to oppose the granting of licenses in Frenchtown. E.G. Williams was chosen as vice-president, Reverend D.M. Matthews as secretary and John R. Hardon as treasurer. In 1879, this organization had 204 members. The Middle Hotel became the Temperance Association's home, as it served as a meeting hall and made an effort to abide by a code of sobriety for its staff and guests. This hotel was destroyed in the fire of 1878.

It is interesting to look comparatively at the borough expenses over time. Initially, Hunterdon County was the most populous county in the state. With the passing of time, the drift of population turned toward the bigger cities, and consequently, there were fewer inhabitants in the countryside. For example, in the first state census, taken in 1737, when the county itself was much larger in area than today, the population was 5,288. This figure was greatly increased by the time of the first United States census in 1790, the figure then being 20,153. In the next eighty years, the population almost doubled, and in the

1870 census, 36,963 people were tallied in the county. However, sixty years later, only 34,728 remained. The county has grown since then, with a good portion being due to bedroom communities for those who work farther east, with the estimated population in 2010 being close to 170,000.

The population of Frenchtown in 1875 was approximately 960, about 1,100 in 1895 and, in the census of 1930, the count was 1,189. In 2012, the population of Frenchtown was close to 1,370, down slightly from the 1,490 counted in the 2000 census.

Listing of Frenchtown Borough Expenditures from 1882 to 2012

Budget Sections	Year		
	1882	1932	2012
Support of Poor	$350	$400	
Officer Salaries and expenses	$430	$1,100	$191,695
Interest on Bonds/notes	$24	$125	$30,966
Principal on Bonds/notes	$400	$2,500	$90,000
Loans principal and Interest			$29,089
Laying Sidewalks	$200		
Street Lighting		$3,300	$21,000
Roads and Streets	$175	$4,000	$232,555
Elections		$250	$1,500
Printing, Insurance, Etc.		$600	$164,382
Maintenance of Hall		$200	$10,000
Auditing		$100	$15,300
Tax Assessment			$10,405
Legal Services/Court Expenses	$50	$50	$118,600
Telephone		$27	$15,800
Electricity			$13,000
Fuel Oil/gas/natural gas			$47,000
Fire Department		$450	$45,762
Police Department			$290,739
Water/ for Fire		$1,447	$1,300

Budget Sections	Year		
	1882	1932	2012
Health Department		$100	$23,418
Unemployment Relief		$300	
Dependency Relief		$100	
Contingent	$450	$200	
Deficiency		$165	
N.J. League of Municipalities		$50	$29,181
Public/private green programs		$25	$68,766
Sewer Utility			$582,337
Education/Public Library		$300	$11,200
Patriotic Observances		$100	
Parks/Recreation/public events			10,000
Approximate Totals	$2,079.00	$15,899.07	$2,309,000*

*The numbers for 2012 are approximations and/or a combination of several different categories.

A comparison of these three budgets (taking out inflationary factors, etc.) helps to show the modern complexities of life. The wide gulf between the budgets is more apparent when the assessed value of property over the years is factored in. This comparison also indicates that money appropriated for streets and street lighting in 1932 constituted almost half the entire budget, while today it is closer to 10 percent of the yearly budget.

The Panic of 1873

The panic of 1873 was one of the worst financial calamities to have hit the United States up to this time. On one Saturday there had been large payrolls, work was abundant and the workers for the most part were well paid and happy. Business was good. However, a very different scene was on the canvas when another payday rolled around. Railroad building from ocean to ocean had brought overexpansion. So long as Europe could lend money to meet the needs of the builders, everything worked well. But when further loans became nonexistent there was no money to continue the pyramiding that was going on, and then came the crash.

To the astonishment of the world, the great banking house of Jay Cook & Company, of Philadelphia, closed its doors. Cook was the famous financier responsible for placing the government's bonds in the hands of the public during the dark days of the Civil War.

When Fargo wrote *History of Frenchtown* (1933), the country was still in the throes of the Great Depression. This had begun in the summer of 1929 and was soon followed by the stock market crash of October 1929. The decline in American stock prices continued until they hit bottom in July 1932, and in the first quarter of 1933, the banking system broke down: asset prices had collapsed, bank lending had largely ceased, a quarter of the American work force was unemployed and real GDP per capita in 1933 was 29 percent below its 1929 value. "But," states Fargo, "bad as things may appear, Frenchtown has not yet reached the state that it found itself in during the 1873 period."

Following the panic of 1873, the winter of 1875 was severely cold; there was still a great scarcity of work and much suffering among the local families. In order to furnish some relief, the Frenchtown Benevolent Society was organized. The altruistic work of this society was continued until late winter of 1877, when the sun began to shine once more, and the society, having fulfilled its purpose, was dissolved.

The Great Fire of 1878

An inferno the likes of which the town had never seen struck Frenchtown on June 29, 1878. It was a Saturday morning, just a few minutes before one o'clock, when the terrifying cries of "Fire! Fire!" were heard in the still night air. Before the sun crept over the horizon at dawn, the heart of the business section lay in ruins.

The fire started in Dr. E.K. Deemy's barn, which was behind the stone house next to Cornelius Hoff's three-story brick building on Harrison Street, and in less than two hours, six dwellings and no less than twenty-one businesses had burned. Almost the entire downtown was in ashes. The cause of the fire was never discovered, but it was thought that possibly a cigar butt or a match inadvertently thrown into the straw started the blaze. Of course, someone's malicious attempt to destroy property could never be completely ruled out either. Among the businesses destroyed were the hub and spoke mills, the Union National Bank, a bed-bottom factory, the American Hotel and its barns and the Frenchtown *Press* establishment.

The conflagration ate its way southward down the east side of Harrison toward Bridge Street, where a two-and-a-half-story frame building owned by A.P. Williams stood. The corner of the building was occupied by George W. Hummer as a furniture and undertaker establishment. Next to Hummer, in the same building, Williams operated a drugstore. Several businesses occupied the upper story, and in the rear, along Harrison Street, there was a string of four small shops. These were all food for the flames, as was the building of Levi Able on Bridge Street, next to the Williams property. The structure that stands today was built for A.L. Williams immediately after the fire. This building (29–39 Bridge Street) is usually called the Hummer Block, although Hummer never owned it.

The flames also leaped to the west side of Harrison Street and struck the American Hotel (Temperance House). The hotel was quickly consumed. The conflagration destroyed the rest of the hotel property north to the alley, which was occupied by the pioneer Frenchtown newspaper the *Press* and a meat shop. The flames also took Samuel Pittinger's barn and continued westward down the alley, destroying sheds and barns down to the intersecting alley and northward into the surrounding homes.

The Vigilant Fire Engine Company No. 1 had one hand engine, which was soon disabled, so heroic measures and quick actions were in order. Bucket brigades, ropes, ladders, old and new carpets and whatever else could be used came into play, along with calls for help. Mayor Haring sent a dispatch at 1:14 a.m. to Lambertville saying, "Send us an engine quick!" The Union Fire Company responded at once. The company loaded its engine and firemen on a flatcar and made the sixteen-mile run in the remarkable time of only nineteen minutes.

The mayor also dispatched a message to Phillipsburg, saying, "Send an engine quick; whole town on fire!" For some reason, there was a delay in replying to this message, but finally, at 3:20 a.m., a reply came that the Phillipsburg and Easton Companies had their equipment loaded and were ready to come. To this message, Bryan Hough, the station agent, replied, "Will not need engines; fire under control now."

In two short hours, the fire had run its course. Due to the heroic work of the citizens, however, total disaster was prevented. Despite many difficulties, they prevented the spread of flames. The fire was an appalling financial loss for those times, in the neighborhood of $50,000, and a number of family men's jobs were literally burned to the ground. Fortunately, there were no casualties, and the buildings on the south side of Bridge Street were saved.

It seems unthinkable today that, for many years, the town was without any fire protection other than what could be given by citizens formed into volunteer bucket brigades like in 1878. Efforts had been made prior to 1878 to establish a volunteer fire company. A meeting was held on February 1, 1866, but no action was taken, and the matter lapsed. Two years later, Vigilant Fire Engine Company No. 1 was organized, and a secondhand, hand-pumped engine was purchased. Silas Wright was president and Garret L. Peer was foreman of the first company when the fire of 1878 occurred. The next attempt at the organization of a fire company was that of the Active Fire Company, organized on November 8, 1883. This company had eighteen active members.

The Union Fire Engine Company No. 1 was organized in 1888, and on March 13, 1889, it was incorporated for a term of fifty years, with a membership of seventy-two. During Wilbur Slack's term as mayor, a new efficient engine—operated by steam, which was *tres moderne* at the time—was purchased at a cost of $1,900.00. In 1924, an updated gasoline-driven engine mounted on an automobile chassis was purchased at a cost of $7,112.50.

Together with the installation of a fire alarm system composed of boxes, located at a number of convenient corners about town and connected to an electric siren mounted in the cupola of the town hall, fire protection at the time was equal to any other up-to-date town, other than cities of a size where they had a paid organization.

NEWSPAPERS

The first newspaper published in Hunterdon County was the *Hunterdon Gazette and Farmer's Weekly Advertiser*, started by Charles George on March 24, 1825. In Frenchtown, before the 1878 fire, there was a dance hall with horse sheds underneath it on Harrison Street. The hall was turned into a printing plant, and Charles Joiner's weekly, the *Press*, was published there until the fire. A single issue was printed in Trenton immediately after the fire, but the publication was subsequently discontinued. The first issue of the *Press* was dated April 2, 1868.

The next to appear in Frenchtown was the *Hunterdon Independent*. The first issue of this newspaper was dated May 5, 1871. It was published by Silvanus

D. and Ross Slack and owned by Andrew Slack. The next owner was John R. Hardon, who continued the publication for many years, finally, in his old age, transferring ownership of the *Independent* to Joshua Stout. Later, the paper passed into the hands of Morgan T. Davy. Ross Slack also began publication of the *Enterprise* on February 11, 1881, but this venture was short-lived, going on for only a few issues before being discontinued.

In 1879, William H. Sipes began printing the *Frenchtown Star*, a small, eight-page monthly that cost twenty-five cents a year. The first issue measured six and a quarter by nine and a half inches. Later, the publication was changed into a six-column, eight-page weekly newspaper and issued continuously up to Sipes's death. Publication was continued for a while under the supervision of his son, Horace E. Sipes. The *Hunterdon County Democrat* purchased the *Frenchtown Star* in 1932 and renamed it the *Delaware Valley News*. The *Delaware Valley News* continued to go to press until the early twenty-first century.

FRENCHTOWN AT THE END OF A CENTURY

One can visualize changes in Frenchtown by viewing an old print showing the town as it was in 1883. On the river are several large rafts of logs on their way downstream to the various sawmills situated along its banks. The

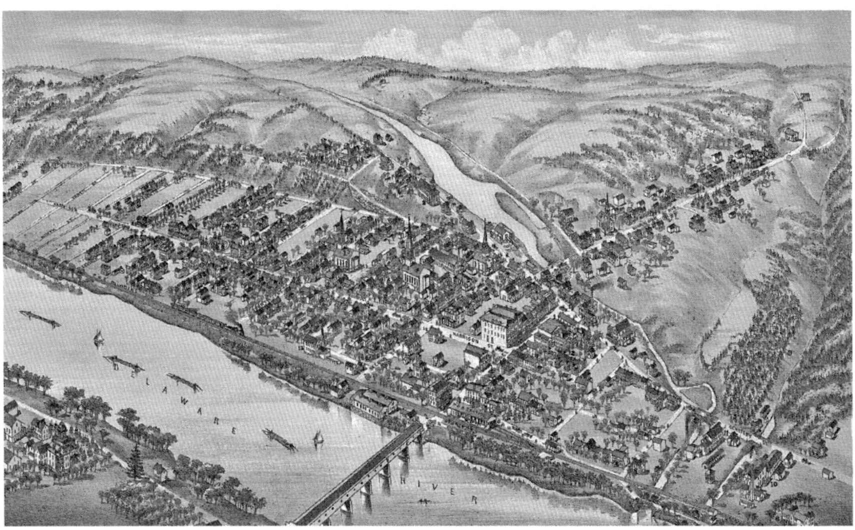

A map of Frenchtown in 1883. *Courtesy of David Miller.*

old covered wooden bridge, completed in 1844, and some homes on the Pennsylvania side of the river are clearly visible, as is the old spoke mill located between Second and Third Streets and Hillside Academy on Everittstown Hill.

One building not on this print is the Odd Fellows Building (17 Bridge Street). At the time that the map was created, only cellar holes and ruined foundations existed on some downtown plots, relics of the great fire of 1878. The Union National Bank had already been completed and appears with vacant lots on either side. The Odd Fellows service organization built the building now standing directly adjacent to the bank.

Odd Fellows—which stands for Independent Order of Odd Fellows, sometimes abbreviated IOOF—is still a global, altruistic and benevolent fraternal organization derived from the British Oddfellows society of the seventeenth century. Where the name Odd Fellows came from is hard to say, but the story goes that in seventeenth-century England it was unusual, or just odd, to find people organized for the purpose of giving aid to those in need. Citizens who belonged to such an organization may have been thought of as odd fellows.

On March 2, 1847, Magnolia Lodge No. 57 of IOOF came into being, with twenty-one charter members, and in 1897, the lodge erected its fine

The majestic Independent Order of Odd Fellows (IOOF) Building on Bridge Street. *Courtesy of Shannon O'Connell.*

three-story brick building on Bridge Street. This undertaking proved an excellent investment. Together with other philanthropic organizations, they occupied the third floor, while the second floor was a great, high-ceilinged, undivided hall. The hall was used for club functions and other public events.

There were numerous benevolent orders and social clubs in and around Frenchtown, including Shepherd's Star Lodge, the Improved Order of Red Men society, the Freemasons and the Lions Club, the latter two still very active today.

The 1883 map also depicts the old stone bridge across Nishisakawick Creek opposite the National Hotel and the vacant lots on the south side of upper Fifth Street with but two houses from the corner of Harrison Street up to Milford Road. Likewise, the south side of upper Seventh and the north side of lower Eighth Streets were then vacant lots, as was Harrison Street above Eighth. The illustration also shows a number of other changes of interest that have occurred from the late 1800s to the mid-1900s.

In the late 1800s, George W. Hayes kept a drugstore on Race Street, as did Albert P. Williams on Bridge Street. Williams's establishment was next to Hummer's furniture store. Williams also manufactured a liniment known as William's Magnetic Relief, a preparation that had many sales in various

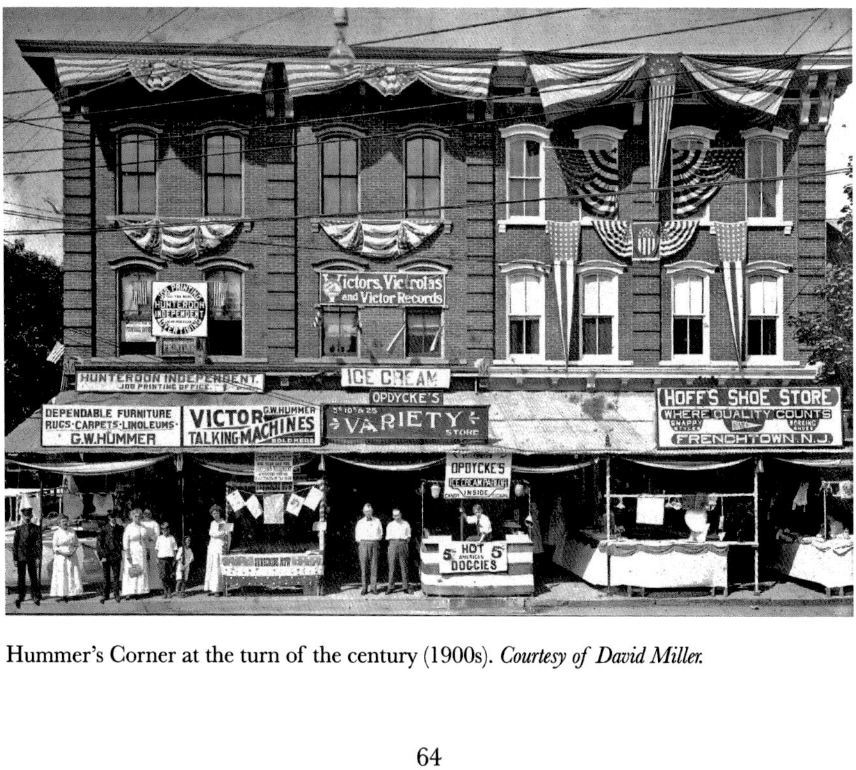

Hummer's Corner at the turn of the century (1900s). *Courtesy of David Miller.*

localities. This was before the fire of 1878. After the fire, the building was rebuilt and kept the name Hummer's Corner. A former state senator, William H. Martin, kept a general store known as the Regulator and later sold out to Dr. J.S. and Charles A. Manners. S. Chester Opdyke later occupied this location, selling ice cream and hot dogs.

Ishmael Brink had a hardware store in the building located at 24–26 Bridge Street that was later occupied by an A&P (Atlantic and Pacific Tea Company). Two other hardware stores were present in town, one run by Charles B. Higgins, which later was operated by the Trimmer family, and the other by Charles C. Webster in the Eddy block. Squire William T. Strope had his office in the back of Webster's store.

In a row of old buildings on Bridge Street, Benjamin Everitt and his son Charles operated a store that sold flour and feed, and Maria Wright kept a small confectionery shop (now the confectionery store Minette's Candies is found at 43 Bridge Street). A tinsmith shop was in what is now the remodeled western end of the Eddy building, and "Captain" Britton, father of Daniel D. and George M., had a livery stable at the National Hotel.

Minette's Candies on Bridge Street—for those who love their sweets. *Courtesy of Brokaw Photography.*

Bridge Street under a blanket of snow in the early 1900s. *Courtesy of David Miller.*

From a very small beginning in 1877, the Britton brothers succeeded in building up the largest and most up-to-date department store (Britton Brothers) in Hunterdon County. One of the brothers, Daniel D., started as an agent for sewing machines, while the other, George M., learned the trade of harness making. Their first location was in an old stone building on Kingwood Avenue. From there, they moved to part of a small, one-story frame building on Race Street, just around the corner from Bridge. Next, they moved to a store that was later operated by E.C. Johnson & Son as a hardware and plumbing store. Then, after the death of Hugh E. Warford, they purchased the three-story brick store at 10 Bridge Street (Gem building). In the early days of the Gay Nineties, Britton Brothers moved to this location amid predictions of disaster, because as many surmised, the store was too far from the business center. With full confidence, however, the brothers added clothing to their store, as well as popular five- and ten-cent counters down the center of the front section of the store, and optimistically opened their doors for business. The truth of the old adage that states "if you do something better than it has been done before, the world will beat a path to your door," was amply proven at Britton Brothers. Here was a store like nothing Frenchtown had ever seen. People flocked to the new store, and it prospered from the start. In later years, however, there came the automobile, and with it, business drifted into larger towns and cities. After the brothers passed away, their business was eventually sold by their heirs to Wilmot Milbury.

It was a small world back then, as it is today. Clarence Fargo was not only related to William Fargo of Pony Express and Wells, Fargo & Co. fame but also received his first business training at Britton Brothers when the store was at its peak. His first job was unpacking dry goods on a single Saturday

A Britton Brothers advertisement. Reaching out to your customers through advertisement is always the key to retail sales. *Courtesy of Rick Epstein, from the Gloria Sipes Paleveda Collection.*

afternoon. Then, a steady job every Saturday afternoon, not because the boss said so but because the boy just appeared on the scene and went right to work. As Clarence's summer vacation was approaching, the boss asked him if he would like a steady summer job. In reply to an affirmative answer, the manager asked how much the boy would expect to be paid. Clarence bid low, $1.50 per week. He was hired on the spot and sold nearly $1,000 worth of goods during the eight weeks of his summer vacation, which made a mighty low overhead for the proprietors. The job was a good learning experience for the boy.

THE GAY NINETIES

If one dug up some of the old, dust-covered photos of the Gay Nineties era, one would, without doubt, laugh, as would anyone twenty years in our future laugh at whatever is in vogue today. In the 1890s, both men and women presented themselves in what we would consider interesting styles today. The ladies decked themselves in picture hats, puffing out their hair with an abundance of rats in order to provide an adequate foundation. These rats were not what we refer to in our day as rattails. In the 1890s, rats were made from hair pulled out of one's brush, stored away until enough was gathered and then bundled together with a hair net into a needed shape—presto, a hair rat was formed. Full flowing skirts were also plentiful in those days, and these, besides being comfortable and stylish, also helped the town by sweeping the sidewalks clean as the owner sashayed down the street. High choker collars and mutton-leg sleeves were also de rigueur of those times.

On Sundays during the 1890s, there were no trains during the day and, consequently, no Sunday newspapers. People went to church for diversion, if for no better purpose, and many couples strolled down to the train station around nine o'clock in the evening to watch the first train of the day roll in. The rate of pay for unskilled labor varied from ninety cents to one dollar and fifty cents per day, often with only two or three days a week work. Mystery of mysteries, some men kept their families together and out of debt with these wages.

The highest-paid man in the town was the bank cashier, who drew $1,200 to $1,500 per annum. Not more than one or two other individual employees in the place received so much as $15 per week, but they considered it more than enough. The rate of pay for carpenters was $2.50 for a ten-hour workday, while masons received $3 per day.

Frequently, one could buy a home for $500 to $900 or rent a very presentable place for anywhere from $3 to $5 per month. In our time, one would be lucky to find a good rental property for $1,000 or so per month.

If one possessed a fortune of $50,000, he or she was considered wealthy beyond the dreams of material comfort, and $20,000 was an amount on which a man with family might comfortably retire. Surely, those were the days of simple living—those Gay Nineties.

6

TURN-OF-THE-CENTURY FRENCHTOWN

In fits and starts, the town continued to grow and change, with the end of the nineteenth century being more a fit than start. The developments planned by Slater & Hudnit fizzled out so that, by 1870, the area north of Eighth Street remained relatively undeveloped. Even with the establishment of the railroad connection, many industries had simply passed by Frenchtown to set up elsewhere, and while the Gay Nineties came and went, only minor changes in appearance or activity were noted. However, the twentieth century brought several transformations in economic focus that really spurred growth and development in the region.

In 1909, the Frenchtown Porcelain Works came to town. The Porcelain Company was headed by Herbert Sinclair of Trenton until he passed away in 1931. Frank Gardner, also from Trenton, took over operations in the 1930s. The company purchased a tract of land between Harrison Street and the railroad and started building operations. In 1910, it began to manufacture spark plugs and porcelain specialties for electrical and plumbing works. Additional land was later purchased, and the tract extended from Eighth to Twelfth Streets. At full capacity, employment at this plant was in the neighborhood of 150 hands. With its financial strength and the jobs it brought to the community, the Porcelain Works contributed to the development of Harrison Street between Tenth and Eleventh Streets.

Two other industries had a hand in early twentieth-century growth: the establishment of the Milford plant of the Warren Paper Company (one of the largest manufacturers of glassine paper in the world) and the spectacular rise of the poultry industry. As big as the paper company was, the hatchery business was a more home-grown affair and, thus, became very influential in the region's growth, and much of the rise of the poultry industry was due to the pioneering role of Kerr Chickeries.

In 1907, Richard W. Kerr began hatching chickens at Kerr Chickeries, Inc. As the demand for baby chicks increased through judicious advertising and customer satisfaction, the business grew. In addition to the original hatchery, a big modern frame structure was erected in 1926 directly across from the train station. In addition to owning hatcheries in Frenchtown; Syracuse, New York; and Springfield, Massachusetts, Kerr also operated retail stores in fifteen separate communities. Kerr Chickeries also had a modern poultry farm located on Everittstown Hill. Incubator capacity at one point reached 1,250,000 eggs, and maximum seasonal employment grew to almost one hundred people. The Kerr family also operated a coal and ice business, with large ice ponds and three large icehouses located north of the borough.

As the industry grew, the chicken business became specialized, with some entrepreneurs running hatcheries while others fattened chickens for market or increased their laying hens. Some switched to larger fowl, concentrating on turkeys. Many Frenchtown residents wanted to get in on the action, and in 1923, more than three million chicks were sent by mail from the Frenchtown post office. Through the 1940s, the industry continued to grow. Some of the larger hatcheries, besides Kerr Chickeries, were run by William F. Hillpot, Elden E. Cooley and Trimmer and Hinkle.

Elden Cooley was a pioneer in the hatching of baby chicks. He started in a small way in 1897, but his business eventually grew until he operated hatcheries in Frenchtown, Trenton and Bridgeville, Delaware. He also managed a wholesale gasoline business in Trenton. Hillpot came on the scene a bit later (1912) but operated a large hatchery in Frenchtown too and expanded operations to a second hatchery in Easton, Pennsylvania. He operated three additional retail stores and also a plant at Des Moines, Iowa. Trimmer and Hinkle were even later on the scene, having purchased a property along Everittstown Road and erected a hatching plant in 1931.

Other business of the day included a global seed business run by Clarence B. Fargo. Clarence was involved in many different ventures, one of which involved shipping flower seeds, bulbs, plants and trees to every quarter of the globe from his establishment located at Seventh and Harrison Streets. The customer who was located the farthest away from Frenchtown lived in the heart of "Darkest Africa," 125 miles from the nearest railroad and a six-day journey from the nearest white neighbors. This customer in Africa was an

American woman who originally hailed from the state of Ohio. It was not unusual for shipments of roses or other plants to be made to far off locales such as India, Korea and Japan.

Paul Cronce also sold seeds, bulbs and so on, from his Kingwood Avenue location under the name Rose Hills Floral Sales. Edward Lott, located on South Harrison Street, also operated a greenhouse for flower plants and hotbeds for vegetable plants, as did James R. Vansycle on Baptistown Road. E.B. Hummer also dealt in potted plants and cut flowers and conducted a real estate agency on the side when he wasn't busy operating as the local justice of the peace.

THE FIRST AUTOMOBILES

One morning in 1904, Frenchtown was awash with the news that "Cornelius Hoff had purchased an automobile and it [was] being unloaded at the depot." The populace rushed quickly to Front Street to see the wonderful horseless carriage, or gasoline buggy. It was the wonder

Early Days of the Automobile. In this photo, an auto is pulling International Harvester equipment. The procession is passing the Martin residence on the corner of Harrison and Bridge Streets. Note Hummer's Corner in the background. *Courtesy of David Miller.*

and envy of all, but in retrospect, it was just a one-lung Oldsmobile runabout that steered with a handle instead of a wheel. It was, however, the most widely sold car of those days.

There were no improved roads nearer than Easton or Trenton in the early days of the automobile. Tires were manufactured with only bicycle experience behind them, and consequently, there was always tire trouble. As Fargo told us in *History of Frenchtown*, "A three thousand mile guarantee was considered liberal and few tires lived up to the full letter of the guarantee." Today, it is not unusual for tires to be guaranteed to last for runs of 30,000 to 100,000 miles.

Not to be outdone (remember, things moved much slower in those days), in early 1907, Clarence Fargo embarked on the adventure of purchasing a car. At the same time, Dr. F.H. Decker also purchased a car; both cars were previously owned. Dr. Decker's purchase was a two-cylinder Queen touring car, while Fargo's was a four-cylinder 1904 Franklin runabout. In an unpublished memoir Fargo was writing, he describes his purchase as "somewhat of a lemon although the purchase price had been the modest sum of $250." Dr. Decker, we are told by Fargo, eventually purchased nineteen different cars, and by the time Fargo had finished writing *History of Frenchtown* in the early 1930s, he claims there were perhaps one and a half to two cars to every home in Frenchtown. Apparently, as some things change, per capita car ownership doesn't.

Lights and Other Modern Conveniences

Modernization of Frenchtown infrastructure started with the waterworks. On September 6, 1900, a franchise was granted for the laying of water mains in the streets of the borough, the installation of fireplugs and water service to the community. Out-of-town interest put the project through and later sold the plant to local businessmen, among them Charles N. Reading, Abel B. Haring, Albert P. Williams and others. This public improvement project was put in during the administration of Mayor Samuel O. Eddy.

Along with improvements in the water supply, the town was moving into the modern age with the advent of a continuous supply of electricity. This process started when a borough franchise was granted to Barnabas Devitt on March 3, 1904. A power plant was installed in the Worman Mill on Trenton Avenue and a limited type of service given. Then an ordinance was passed for the building and operation of a municipal electric light plant on November 1, 1906. Dr. J.S. Manner was mayor at this time.

A plant was erected on a plot of ground purchased from James E. Sherman across from the train depot, and a street lighting service was then provided, as well as a limited house service. No current was available for daytime use. Over time, a proposition to sell the plant and franchise to private interests appeared on the horizon. On September 3, 1925, the borough council approved it. The voters at an election held on November 3 of the same year approved the ordinance; 328 affirmative and only 76 negative.

The State Board of Public Utilities had advised the sale, provided at least $20,000 could be secured, if not more. The sale was consummated at a price of $31,500, and the plant passed into the hands of the New Jersey Power & Light Company, a link in the chain of the Associated Gas and Electric System.

Today, telephones seem to be attached from birth, so who would believe it took some getting used to? But early telephones did. They were very noisy, not extremely efficient and scared the farm animals. But with much promotion, the technology did catch on. "Talk to someone in another town all day if you want to" was announced in the *Hunterdon County Democrat* on September 15, 1885. What was the paper promoting? A simple hookup between Lambertville and Flemington by an affiliate of the Bell Telephone Company.

Of course, like most new technologies, the cost was high, and this is why local telephone companies were started to compete with the high rates charged by Bell. Companies such as the Farmers and Merchants Telephone Company and the Lebanon Telephone Company built lines throughout Hunterdon County. The Farmers and Merchants Telephone Company built the communication lines connecting Frenchtown, Lambertville, Flemington and Clinton and points in between. The rates these companies charged were low, but the out-of-town service was poor. In time, three different local companies brought lines into Flemington, making it necessary to have three different telephones in one's home if one wanted complete service. Fortunately, the three companies were consolidated in 1931, but later on, this organization sold out to New Jersey Telephone Company. While the rates for local service were considerably higher, the service was improved, and quick connections with all long distance points became available, even with overseas connections like London, Paris or Berlin if one was willing to pay the high cost. In Frenchtown, the telephone company no longer makes use of the beautiful three-story converted home it once occupied; instead, its operations are nestled into a one-story brick bunker at the corner of Second and Harrison Streets.

The beautiful home that was used by the Telephone Exchange has been torn down, and now the telephone company makes use of a nondescript one-story brick building. *Courtesy of David Miller.*

THE FRESHET OF 1903

Life along the river can bring hardships, especially when water moves up onto what is normally dry land. A freshet is a sudden overflowing of a stream because of melting snow or heavy rain, usually from a spring thaw. Another definition of freshet is, simply, a flood.

For three days in the early part of October 1903, the Delaware began to rapidly rise due to steady and continuous rain, and soon it had become sullen and menacing, overflowing its banks and encroaching on the right-of-way of the railroad—even flooding the lower ends of some of the cross streets in Frenchtown. The flood soon drew the populace to the riverbanks along the railroad, particularly to the vicinity of the train station and the river bridge, the safety of the latter becoming seriously threatened.

During the rapid rise of the waters, James Crosby of the Crosby Manufacturing Company attempted to cross the swollen torrent in his gasoline launch from a point near Sixth Street, but misjudging the strength of the current, he was unable to make the Pennsylvania shore to the north of the bridge and, when passing under the structure, was only able to save himself by ducking down into the boat. He was lucky there was just enough room between the surface of the water and the bottom of the bridge for the boat to pass safely. It took a while, but he was finally able to get back to the Jersey shore near the mouth of the Nishisakawick.

At the height of the flood, the waters completely covered the railroad tracks and washed over the platform of the depot, the highest the river had risen since the great freshet of 1841. The 1841 flood had washed away all existing bridges between Easton and Trenton.

When the waters had somewhat receded in 1903, there remained a picture of desolation. Across from the icehouse, the railroad tracks hung in a great loop over the side of the stone embankment, reminding one of a giant lace festoon. The last train to arrive at Frenchtown was on late Saturday afternoon, October 10, and railroad service was at a complete standstill until the following Friday. For six days, Frenchtown and other points along the train line were cut off from the rest of the world outside—even the mail had to wait on the resumption of train service.

Between Easton and Trenton, the only intact bridge was the one at Stockton. The bridge at Riegelsville was entirely swept away by the

The bridge keeper's house of 1906 no longer exists. In this photo is the repaired bridge, which had two steel spans connecting to the wooden remainder of the original structure. *Courtesy of David Miller.*

flood, and those at Milford and Lumberville each lost one span, while the Frenchtown Bridge lost two. While awaiting the necessary repairs to the Frenchtown Bridge, the resourceful citizens returned to days of yore and stretched a wire cable across the river above the old foundry property and built a flat-bottomed ferry, with James Gray in charge as ferryman. The ferry was used to carry both foot passengers and wagons. This served until the covered wooden bridge was patched up with two steel spans replacing those destroyed by the freshet. It became a bit of an eyesore but was still a valuable asset and a necessity for the community.

Pennsylvania and New Jersey, through the Joint Bridge Commission, gradually began purchasing the toll bridges spanning the Delaware, improving them or building new bridges and making them free to traffic. The repaired bridge at Frenchtown was purchased by the Joint Commission at a cost of $45,000.00 and opened as a free bridge. This bridge was later replaced after repairs were made to the piers and abutments, the tollhouse was remodeled and an entire new superstructure was built. The new bridge cost $91,510.87 in addition to the original purchase price of the old structure. Appropriate dedicatory exercises were held in Frenchtown on Saturday afternoon, October 10, 1931, exactly twenty-eight years to the day after the destruction of the two old wooden spans by the angry waters of the freshet of 1903.

FRENCHTOWN AT PLAY

When they weren't busy working or improving the town's infrastructure, Frenchtowners enjoyed a variety of recreational and leisure activities. Locals could be found boating and fishing along the river as well as enjoying novel pastimes such as the moving pictures.

The old penny arcades and the nickelodeon largely passed out with the coming of the movies. The first moving pictures were very crude, flickered badly, were a real trial to the eyes and were usually shown in some vacant storeroom at an admission of a dime. At first, the pictures had no plot or story, being simply horses racing, men fighting or other scenes of animated action. They were still a sensation, just as the radio was in a later day. As time passed, the motion pictures were improved and eventually became known as the silent drama. The next step was the talking picture with which we are all familiar.

A young Italian shoemaker came to Frenchtown around 1909, and like many other keen youth, he had his ear close to the ground, listening for the cooing of opportunity. This young man's name was Peter de Mauro, and it was by his initiative that the first movie theater was opened in Frenchtown. This theater doubled as the town hall. Mauro sold out his interest to William F. Hillpot and departed for other fields. Later, the business passed into the hands of Fred H. Sipes, who moved it to the Worman Building on Bridge Street, purchasing the building after the death of David Worman. After Sipes's French Theatre closed, Wilmot Milbury remodeled a part of his large store building at 10 Bridge Street as the Gem Theatre. It was the finest movie house in Hunterdon County when it opened to the public on Thursday, July 14, 1932. People entered the theater through a side entrance, which is now where Schmidtberger Fine Arts (SFA) sits today.

The entrance to the Gem Theatre in 1932 was through the side of the building. Today, this section of the Gem building is home to SFA. *Courtesy of John Schmidtberger.*

The 1909 baseball team (left side). *Left to right, standing*: Leon A. Park, center field; Frank Pinkerton, short stop; Raymond Bloom, right field; Walter Everitt, left field; Harman "Doc" Slack, substitute; Art Rittenhouse, second base; Walter Rogers, first base; and Jack Everitt, third base. *Left to right, sitting*: George Naylor, pitcher; Robert Hughes, manager; Jack Calton, catcher; and Goose Snyder, pitcher. The 1910 baseball team (right side). *Left to right, standing*: Jack Everitt, third base; Andy Monohau, second base; Leon A. Park, center field; Arthur Rittenhouse, first base; Robert Hughes, manager; Harman "Doc" Slack, substitute; and Frank Pinkerton, short stop. *Left to right, sitting*: Walter Everitt, left fielder; George Naylor, pitcher; George Kline, catcher; Walter Rogers, right field; and Holmes LaRue Jr., mascot. *Courtesy of Rick Epstein, from the Gloria Sipes Paleveda Collection.*

Probably the most enthusiastic of sports days in Frenchtown date to the formation of baseball teams in the early 1900s. The area where the Frenchtown Porcelain Company (Star Porcelain) eventually built its business was used as a diamond; a grandstand was built, and twenty-five cents was charged for admission. Even at this high entrance cost, the Frenchtown team drew large crowds to watch them play teams from Easton, Flemington, Lambertville, Milford and other nearby locales. Enthusiasm ran high, with even more excitement in the air on days when Frenchtown was scheduled to play Milford.

Usually, each team provided itself with a hired battery and frequently with other hired players as well, but the balance of each team was made of local talent. In his book, Fargo highlights one pitcher who seemed to meet with a great deal of success in the box and became a local idol. His name was Naylor, and he hailed from Lambertville. Fans had a popular battle cry for him: "Naylor is a wonder! Milford will go under!" Whether Milford actually did go under, how often and to what extent depends on which town the storyteller hails from these days.

Football teams were also organized in towns along the river and played in Frenchtown and surrounding communities on Saturdays and holidays. One Saturday in particular, there was a game scheduled for Point Pleasant, but the bridge was out. Not to worry—a rowboat met the team on the Jersey side, and everybody piled in so the boatman didn't have to make two trips. It was a close call; the water of the river became almost level with the top of the boat. Fortunately, they arrived at the other side without mishap, and what might have been a tragedy turned out to be a pleasant day.

After the arrival of the Star Porcelain Company, and its purchase of all the real estate on the west side of Harrison Street from Eighth to Twelfth, a modern grandstand was built at the northwestern corner of these grounds and an ideal field for athletes of all sorts was put in. This field is now used for many outdoor activities scheduled for both the school and the town.

Frenchtown even had its own country club for a short time—from 1890 to around 1912. This establishment had a tennis court for town residents, and a private house on upper Fourth Street was purchased for use as a clubhouse. The building still stands and is now home to hardworking citizens of the community, and as the need for housing increased, the tennis court was replaced by another private residence.

THE GREAT WORLD WAR

War clouds were hanging over Europe in 1914, foretelling of the bloodshed to come; nevertheless, the world was shocked when, on August 4, 1914, the German army began a thrust through Belgium in an attempt to quickly reach French soil.

In honor of the first group of boys from Frenchtown to be shipped overseas, an informal banquet was served on the evening of August 31, 1917, at the Warford House. After a bountiful feast, a number of speeches were made and then each soldier was presented with a billfold as a memento of the occasion, with the hope that all would speedily, and safely, return home. Soon after, these men were off for training at Camp Dix. Some eventually saw active service overseas; others were assigned permanently to service on this side of the Atlantic.

On November 11, 1918, the news of the signing of the Armistice was received. Many of us who live in days when the world wars have long passed cannot conceive of the strain global conflicts impose on everyday life. But those living in Frenchtown at that time, as a barometer of the country at large, did feel the pain. The joy that filled men's hearts at the news that the strife and bloodshed had ended was as total as the sorrow for all those who would not

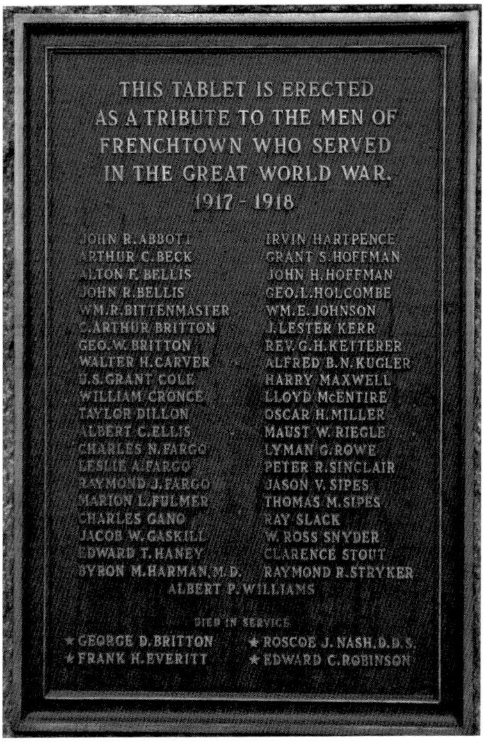

Above: The doughboy statue proudly stands in front of Edith Ort Elementary School on Harrison Street. *Courtesy of Caroline Scutt.*

Right: The plaque beneath the doughboy statue bears the names of those who did and did not return from the war. *Courtesy of Caroline Scutt.*

return. Many who did return were broken in body and mind. Fortunately, the majority was unscathed, but they had gone through an experience that would carry both happy and sad remembrances for the rest of their lives.

A few years later, mayor Dr. Frank Grim called together a committee to consider a fitting memorial, so that present and future generations might do honor to those who had served their country in time of need. At an expense of $2,700, the granite monument, surmounted by the bronze doughboy in action, was erected on the lawn in front of the new school building, and appropriate dedicatory exercises marked the occasion. The committee also had a steel flagpole erected. An appropriation from the borough council and private subscriptions (from fifty cents or one dollar up to several hundred dollars) funded the project. The names of Frenchtown's World War I soldiers and sailors are inscribed on a bronze plate on the front of the granite base.

It should be noted here that Congress chartered the American Legion in 1919 as a patriotic veterans organization. The legion focuses on service to veterans, service members and communities. The legion evolved from a group of war-weary veterans from World War I into one of the most influential nonprofit groups in the United States. Fidelity Post No. 113 was chartered with fifteen members on June 9, 1920. The American Legion Auxiliary of Fidelity Post No. 113 was chartered with forty-seven members on April 25, 1931.

THE FRENCHTOWN CEMETERY

The Frenchtown Cemetery is one of the most beautiful cemeteries to be found in a community the size of Frenchtown. With its old shade trees and its well-kept plots, along with the dates and inscriptions on many of the tombs, it is a peaceful place to contemplate life and study history.

Started as a private burying ground with the interring of Mrs. Mallet-Prevost in 1810, the cemetery was later opened for public use and organized as a cemetery association on September 30, 1857. The association has made several purchases of adjacent tracts, and beneath the cemetery's green sod, the buried remains considerably outnumber those alive in the borough today. Philip G. Reading (1816–86) and W.W. Hedges (1809–79), who were business partners in life, lie within a few feet of each other in death. Beside the old original Mallet-Prevost plot lies Andrew G. Mallet-Prevost (1821–1907), his wife and four children.

Right: At one time, gravestones were made to order right outside the cemetery. *Courtesy of David Miller.*

Below: Another view of the historic Frenchtown Cemetery. *Courtesy of Caroline Scutt.*

The restricted meaning of "elegy" (from the Greek term *elegeia*), as a poem of regret, a lament called forth by the decease of a loved one or other tragic event, has been in place since the sixteenth century. In England, an elegy was considered a component of the inscription for a tombstone since the beginning of the seventeenth century, and many of them are very bizarre, to say the least. To a large extent, the use of the elegy on tombstones passed out of fashion in the mid-1800s, but a short stroll through the older section of the Frenchtown Cemetery affords some examples of this custom of the past.

At least fifteen gravestones were noted that carried the following inscription or an excerpt therefrom:

Asleep in Jesus; blessed sleep,
from which none ever wake to weep.

Advice of an eighteen-year-old daughter to her parents reads like this:

Farewell Father and Mother dear;
I am not dead, but sleeping here.
Prepare for death, for die you must,
And with your daughter sleep in dust.

And this, from a small stone in memory of a child:

We had a little Herby once;
We loved him, ah too well.
The angles came and took him,
To his heavenly home to dwell.

SLOWLY CHANGING LANDSCAPES

Farming shouldn't be overlooked in the discussion of changes in the industrial base throughout the region. In the early twentieth century, Frenchtown and the surrounding area now had the paper, porcelain and poultry industries along with a flourishing plant and nursery business. At the same time, two gristmills continued to operate in Frenchtown: the Worman mill on the site of the original 1750s Alexandria mill and Sunshine Mills in the stone building that had also seen service in the distillery business and as Nathan Shurtz's spoke factory. Farming was still big in all of Hunterdon County through the 1970s. However, over the latter part of the twentieth century, farming diminished in the county due to the rising costs of labor, machinery, raw materials and property values, while overall product value remained stable.

During the 1920s and '30s, the commercial district along Bridge and Race Streets played host to an array of stores offering nearly everything the town (and surrounding region) could need or want. At the heart of Frenchtown was one of the county's largest hardware stores, run by George W. Eddy since 1884. Eddy's large building, built around 1840, housed for a time a Masonic lodge on its third floor. This building had held Frenchtown's major hardware emporium since before the days of Slater & Hudnit and had housed their business before the Eddy family assumed ownership. Competing with Eddy's store in the center of town was the Milbury Atlantic Company; the department store was located in today's Gem building where Britton Brothers had also operated. As stated previously, the Gem building expanded in 1932 to include the town's third movie theater. G.W. Hummer operated a furniture store and undertaking parlor (enterprises that were often paired in the nineteenth and early twentieth centuries) on the corner building that bears his name. Near Hummer's Corner were two ice cream parlors and candy stores.

Other downtown businesses included small hardware stores, the local bank, another department store (this one with a resident tailor), grocers, lawyer offices, a doctor, a dentist and a pharmacy. To round out the offerings in downtown Frenchtown, there were the newspaper publishers and kiosks, the post office, a stove dealer, a plumber, many restaurants and the two remaining hotels, both with saloons. Interestingly, the composition of Frenchtown's downtown businesses is similar today, although that wasn't true in the mid-twentieth century.

Throughout the commercial district, people lived amid the business buildings in single-family houses or in apartments over the stores. In more recent times, single-family homes are no longer found in this part of town (unless you include the side streets), but as in days of yore, many people still do live in apartments throughout the commercial district. On Harrison Street and Kingwood Avenue, two car dealerships were established, and outside the commercial district but not far from the center of town were coal yards and lumberyards. The ice business was still in full swing, centered near a series of small ponds about a mile north of town.

7

A SLEEPY RIVER TOWN BECOMES MODERNIZED

Lois Johnson remembers the 1940s in Frenchtown as a place where children would "run away" down the alley. Her grandmother often sent her to the A&P to get pansies to be planted. Where? Why, in the garden behind the funeral parlor, because that is where her grandparents had a second-floor apartment. Her family owned the W.E. Johnson Funeral Parlor at 41 Bridge Street until the mid-1990s when pressure from the other downtown businesses, along with other considerations, convinced the family to close the business in Frenchtown and focus on their site in Holland Township. Her family lived above the funeral parlor for a time and then resided in a Victorian home at 112 Harrison Street. They lived next door to a similar dwelling where the phone company occupied the third floor—until, that is, the bland brick box that stands there today replaced it.

As carefree as life can be at one moment, more serious events are never far off. In the 1940s, Frenchtown life was punctuated by two major occurrences that are impossible for those who lived through them to forget: on the global stage, another world war began; locally, on one night in April 1940 on Bridge Street, a massive fire engulfed the hardware store owned by George W. Eddy II, the grandson of George W. Eddy.

Lois Johnson, who lived across the street, vividly remembers being just a toddler when her big brother woke her up. "He kicked me in the stomach to get me up! The fire lasted so long mom served tea and sandwiches to the fire fighters and neighbors."

This was once the home of longtime resident Lois Johnson. *Courtesy of Rick Epstein, from the Gloria Sipes Paleveda Collection.*

The fire raged through the three-story Eddy building, and part of the roof collapsed. Eleven fire companies and nine fire engines were on the scene. There was concern that the underground oil tank feeding the gas pumps in front of the building would explode. Johnson can still hear "the firemen telling my mother to pack us up and be ready to evacuate. That was scary for all of us." Rumor has it that sparks from a floor sander started the fire, but the official cause listed was spontaneous combustion.

Eddy's hardware store was rebuilt by the end of the year, and attention had turned to the new Tower Craftsman Company, which had moved into a factory on Sixth Street. The company manufactured lamps, giftware and furniture and would, at times, employ up to sixty local residents. When the United States officially entered World War II, the factory manufactured defense materials instead of giftware, as did the Frenchtown Porcelain Plant on Eighth Street.

The homefront was also very busy. The townspeople collected scrap metal, and food and gas rationing was implemented to support the wartime efforts, causing a great reduction in automobile travel. The Frenchtown Women's Club sent packages containing fruitcakes, cheese, candy, toothpaste and even copies of the *Delaware Valley News* to all the local men and women in service around the world.

GAS
SUNOCO
OIL
Coca-Cola
KITCHEN

GAS
SUNOCO
OIL

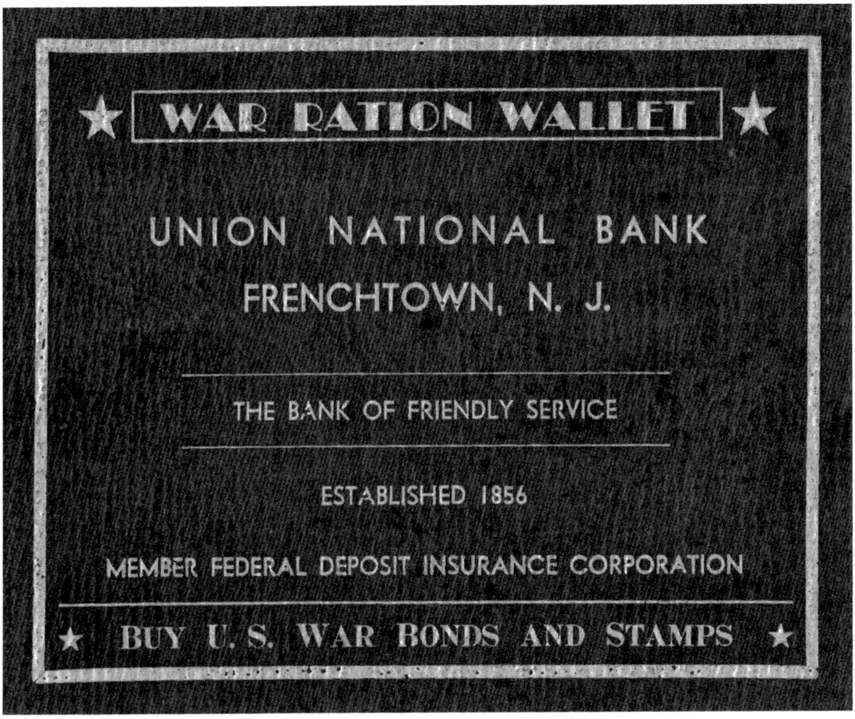

Above: Everyone had to tighten their belts on the homefront. *Courtesy of Rick Epstein, from the Gloria Sipes Paleveda Collection.*

Opposite, top: The fire at the Eddy Hardware Store in 1940. In this picture, the fire is beginning to engulf the three-story building. *Courtesy of David Miller.*

Opposite, bottom: The fire attracted a crowd, though the gasoline pump in the front of the building is clearly visible, and it is surprising that these people stood so close. *Courtesy of David Miller.*

Private Herbert W. Howard was the first resident killed during the war in 1943. He was aboard the *Dorchester*, a troop transport ship torpedoed by German U-boats. In all, 132 Frenchtown men and women would serve in World War II.

In the early 1940s, cars weren't yet ubiquitous, and horses were often still used for transportation. There was train service to and from Trenton, and the Blue Line Bus Company introduced bus service between Somerville and Easton via Flemington, Frenchtown and Milford. Easton was a popular shopping and entertainment destination back then and, at this writing, is undergoing a renaissance as young people flock to live there.

The first part of this particular decade also saw the introduction of Frenchtown's first full-time police officer by Mayor Hugh Sinclair, as well as the borough's purchase of the water company. In the postwar period, Frenchtown refocused its energies on the needs of the borough, including a new $7,000 ambulance. The borough council had also begun exploring the option of a new, desperately needed, sewage system, but the price tag of $350,000 put off many residents, so the system wasn't put in place until years later.

Owen B. Kerr, president of Kerr Chickeries, died in July 1947. He had helped shape the town that had fueled his success. Kerr had served as vice-chairman of the Delaware River Joint Toll Bridge Commission, as a director of the First National Bank of Milford, as a director of the Frenchtown Cemetery Association and as a member of the Frenchtown Borough Council.

The Frenchtown-Uhlerstown Bridge closed for repairs at the end of the decade, and Frenchtown remained cut off from its Pennsylvania neighbors for more than two months. The bridge reopened in July 1949, and the event was celebrated with a parade, reopening ceremonies and speeches. One might wonder today what keynote speaker Hunterdon County judge Wesley Lance (father of U.S. congressman Leonard J. Lance) would think about the four thousand vehicles that now cross the bridge daily, according to the count of the Delaware River Joint Toll Bridge Commission.

MID-NINETEENTH-CENTURY CHANGES COME TO FRENCHTOWN

Clarence Fargo was elected president of the Union National Bank of Frenchtown in 1951 and served as the president of the Frenchtown Cemetery Association. In the 1950s, the population growth in Hunterdon County was ahead of the state's overall growth rate. At that time, there was a back-to-the-land movement of urban folks going out to the country with an influx of immigrants joining them. Farming had become more sophisticated, and improved transportation and refrigerated trucks helped the region's farmers to succeed, especially in dairy and poultry, in Hunterdon. However, then, like today, farming in Pennsylvania was even less expensive, and there would soon be a negative impact on Hunterdon agriculture and related businesses, many of which were located in Frenchtown. The automobile would take over the once quiet streets, and the last passenger rail train would roll out of town in October 1960.

Mrs. Trimmer and her daughter, Kathleen, sitting on the railroad tracks, with Kerr Chickeries (Front Street) in the background. *Courtesy of Robert Trimmer.*

The most notable year of the decade was 1955, when the Delaware Valley felt the deadly wrath of Mother Nature again. Hurricane Hazel had hit the valley in November 1954, causing $50,000 of damage, according to Mayor Lynford Miller. Just eight months later, the notorious flood of '55, caused by Hurricane Diane, washed out the valley, leaving behind damage not seen before in the history of the region. When the river crested, it rose two feet above the high flood mark set in Frenchtown by the freshet of 1903. Homes and industries up and down the river were demolished. Guy De Sapio recalls his earliest memory of Frenchtown being of the flood. "I remember my dad taking us here right after the flood and how impressed I was by the water running *over* the bridge."

Lois Johnson also remembers the flood of '55 as being very frightening. "People died or were trapped further north on the river. Our favorite

During the flood of '55, water rose up to the steps at the Frenchtown Inn, and in the background of this photo, one can see where it laid waste to Niece's lumberyard. *Courtesy of Rick Epstein, from the Gloria Sipes Paleveda Collection.*

swimming spot in the creek was washed away—that mattered very much to me as a young child. We all had to get typhoid shots. You knew everyone who was affected. I remember the watermark being up to the ceiling of the first floor at a friend's grandparents' home on Railroad Avenue."

Kerr Chickeries' back-up generator was destroyed, leaving the facility awash with flooded incubators, resulting in a loss of 250,000 hatching eggs and seven thousand chicks. The Frenchtown Feed Mill lost over $2,000 worth of feed. I.L. Niece & Son Lumber Company was left for done because, after the disaster, only a shell of the business remained. Employee Howard John Opdyke took part of the business over, and H.J. Opdyke Lumber Company continues to thrive on the north side of Frenchtown—on much higher ground. The rest is now Niece Lumber (in Lambertville) today.

More than 200 residents were evacuated, and property damage was assessed at $320,000, but none of Frenchtown's residents lost their lives in the disaster. Other communities weren't as fortunate, and 99 people died in the Delaware Valley. The total death toll along the Eastern Seaboard was between 184 and 200, according to Mary A. Shafter, author of the book of record on the flood, *Devastation on the Delaware*. The Delaware Valley waterways would remain relatively calm for almost fifty years until Mother

Tensions were high in 2006 as the waters tried again to reach out and touch the bridge. *Courtesy of Brokaw Photography.*

Nature focused her hurricane-force wrath there in triplicate during the storms of 2004, 2005 and 2006.

Frenchtown closely averted another disaster in 1955 when three young men broke into a freight car filled with dynamite and stole one hundred pounds of explosives. The boys may have thought themselves unlucky to be caught; however, officials on the scene noted that the young men had been smoking while removing the dynamite. One spark or a tossed cigarette would have blown up Kerr Chickeries, the railroad station, Apgar House, the Gem building and the bridge house. This would certainly have rewritten the history of Frenchtown from that moment onward.

The Frenchtown Library moved in 1950 from its cramped space on Harrison to its current location beneath Borough Hall on Second Street. The library had been organized on March 31, 1919, with the Presbyterian minister Reverend Robert L. Logan as president, Catherine Bellis as secretary and Mrs. Cornelius S. Hoff as treasurer. The first librarian was Lizzie Hummer. The library began with books obtained from the State Circulating Library and books that had been used in the soldier training camps during World War I. It was first situated in the corner of the large, second-floor, front room in the brick building on the south side of Bridge Street (32 Bridge Street). This is the building where Okey Pittinger had kept his store that sold "most everything from a needle to a locomotive." These days, the building is still functional, and the law offices of Anthony Danzo use the bottom floor.

The Frenchtown Library was initially supported by $1 membership dues, renewed each year, and additional funds were secured by holding bake sales and other events. At the present time, the borough budget carries an appropriation of $11,200 (see the table on page 58, 2012 budget, education/library), and this appropriation, together with book fines, finances the library. In 1932, the library consisted of about one thousand volumes, which had been acquired through purchase and donation. Nearly ten thousand volumes were circulated during 1931–32, when the official membership was approximately five hundred patrons. The library is now affiliated with the Hunterdon County library system.

Sara Heil, who moved to Frenchtown in 1979, has been the librarian since 1989, when librarian Sophie Sewak retired. "I kept a cheat-sheet under my desk because I didn't know the Dewey-Decimal System well! My kids grew up in this library. All my life I wanted to work in a bookstore. This is my bookstore." The collection of the Frenchtown branch of the library now contains over 10,150 volumes and circulates over 20,499 items per year as it serves a population of close to 1,200 residents. The Frenchtown Public Library is tiny by today's standards but reflective of Frenchtown—a little worn around the edges but well-loved and busy.

In 1952, an extension was put on the Frenchtown Firehouse, located next to Borough Hall, in order to accommodate two fire engines. The Hunterdon Medical Center near Flemington took shape in 1953, and longtime Frenchtown physician Dr. Arthur M. Jenkins was named vice-president. Parking meters in the borough numbered seventy, and although deemed necessary because of the limited space, residents didn't appreciate having to adhere to the parking restrictions (some things never change).

The increase in motor vehicles also contributed to the relocation of the Samuel C. Worman Memorial Fountain from Bridge Street to Borough Park, where it remains today. Worman, a Philadelphia liquor distributor and farm owner near Frenchtown, had the monument and fountain built to be a "public drinking place for man and beast." The fountain was, for a time, considered a beast itself, causing dented fenders on cars, which hastened its relocation to the park.

The rise in car travel also gave way to the completion of another portion of Route 29, then known as the Delaware River Drive, between Stockton and Byram. However, the "road to hell" or "missing link," as the stretch just

Cars were lined up waiting to get onto the hatchery grounds. Behind the mass of automobiles is the Warford House (Frenchtown Inn). To the left is the train station, and across the street from that is the Gem building. *Courtesy of Robert Trimmer.*

south of Frenchtown was called, promised for more than twenty-five years to facilitate travel to Trenton, had remained unfinished until the spring of 1960, when the section between Frenchtown and Byram was completed. Route 29 north of Trenton is now designated as the Delaware River Scenic Byway and is a well-loved tourist route, especially popular with cyclists.

In the early 1950s, downtown Frenchtown was the destination for most shopping needs with three grocery stores, two hardware stores, two car garages/gas stations (with another on Twelfth Street) and two five-and-ten stores (one complete with a shoe repair shop, a bank, a funeral home, a drugstore and several restaurants). Times were a-changin' in the late '50s and early '60s and so did the downtown streetscape in Frenchtown. In 1956, Landis Department Store opened its doors on Race Street along with Doc Slack's Barber Shop in the brick building on the corner of Race and Bridge. Around the same time, a local landmark, the Biledeou Electric Supply Store on Harrison, was demolished. A year later, the American Store in the IOOF Building on Bridge Street closed its doors due to increasing competition from supermarkets.

The Union National Bank acquired the former home of Dr. H.M. Harmon that stood on the corner of Bridge and Harrison and replaced the dilapidated old Victorian with a drive-in area and parking lot for the bank as part of its improvement plan.

There were several popular hangouts around town where one could get a cup of coffee or bite to eat, including the Candy Kitchen in the Eddy building and Soc Hero's doughnut shop at 26 Bridge Street. Farther up Harrison, the Milk House on Twelfth Street and the Puritan Luncheonette on the corner of Eighth and Harrison Streets were popular spots with the high school crowd.

Robert Trimmer's family owned the Puritan from 1950 to 1955. He remembers being a student at the high school, and as soon as they were let out for lunch, he would run across the street to help his parents, William and Elnora, prepare as many as two hundred hamburgers while he was eating his lunch.

The Puritan was still very much on the mind of William Trimmer more than forty years later when he awoke from a dream and wrote down what he could

Robert Trimmer as a young lad in the Puritan, 1954. *Courtesy of Robert Trimmer.*

remember. "Owning the Puritan in Frenchtown was ordained to make me realize I was married to a saint." He attributes the success of the venture to his wife, Elnora. Some of the regulars who visited the Puritan were Arnie Cochran, Dick Fleck, Harvey Stout, Donald Crouse, Don Hampton, Gretta Rockafellow and two employees, Marion Purcel and Esther (Ellie) Frankenfield. A dip of ice cream was five cents but cost over eight cents to make. "Any money that was made, which wasn't much, was made in the kitchen. We made a living. Long hours and hard work," William recalled in later years. Robert Trimmer followed his parents' example and worked at several jobs in the hatcheries and main office for Kerr Chickeries before changing hats and enlisting in the air force.

During the 1950s, events in the outside world—the Korean Conflict, the rise of the Cold War, Hawaii and Alaska joining the United States and even the growing use of television—were less intrusive on Frenchtown than

Robert Trimmer's father, William, in the Puritan, 1953. *Courtesy of Robert Trimmer.*

the rest of the world, but the town was not entirely immune to the coming changes, which caused the town struggle to define and redefine itself over the next two decades.

Dairy and poultry farms were still the predominant agricultural businesses in Hunterdon County in the early 1960s, but farming evolved as new equipment technology led to cash crop farming that provided for crops such as wheat or soy to be grown, harvested, stored and marketed with minimum labor. These changes were among many taking place in the Delaware River Valley and beyond and would impact life along the river, as would changes in the distribution of the population. By the end of the 1950s, the population shifts brought the last class to graduate from Frenchtown High School, and from then on, the facility became the Edith Ort Thomas Elementary School.

Throughout the Northeast, rust belt communities that had once flourished as coal towns, mill towns, factory towns and market towns would suffer as industries closed down, shrank or moved elsewhere. The nearly three hundred people who worked for Frenchtown's, and the county's, largest employer in 1973, the Porcelain Works, didn't envision the changes over the next ten years that would affect this working-class town. In this regard, a major occurrence took place in 1973 that would have lasting impact on Frenchtown: the fire that devastated Kerr Chickeries' main hatchery on Lott Street.

The fire remains a vivid memory for many Frenchtowners. Kathy McNally Petro was ten years old but remembers every detail of that warm August evening as if it were yesterday. "My brother Don was working at the hatchery that night. The town's fire alarms went off, and my mom and I ran off down the alley between Third and Fourth in the direction of the hatchery. Usually when the fire alarm went off and you wanted to find out where the fire was, you ran down to the fire station to see the address written on a black board, but that day, we could see the smoke coming from the Chickeries. I can still hear my mother saying, 'Oh my God I didn't turn the corn pot off. Run home!'"

After running home to turn off the stove and possibly prevent another fire, ten-year-old Kathy joined the rest of the Frenchtowners who were pressing close to the fire. Her brother and everyone else who'd been in the hatchery were fine, but the building was completely destroyed. The heat emanating from the fire was so hot that the soles of shoes of people who stood on the railroad tracks began to melt. The hatchery was destroyed, and Frenchtown's poultry industry was pretty much incinerated as well.

An aerial view of Kerr Chickeries on Front Street. *Courtesy of Robert Trimmer.*

Kerr moved all operations to its Everittstown Hill poultry farm and greatly reduced its production, which was mainly supplying embryos to New Jersey's growing pharmaceutical industry at that time.

Kathy Petro graduated from Frenchtown Elementary School in 1977 and has been the secretary there for the last twenty years. Like others who grew up there in the '70s and '80s, she doesn't remember the unkempt buildings or remuddled architecture. The Frenchtown she grew up in "had everything you could ever need—park, downtown, Hummers Ice Cream, the Barn Theater, the Frenchtown Roller Rink—everybody came to Frenchtown because we had everything." She also has the distinct honor of having had a parade held for her, because when she was born the sixth of seven children to Jean and Jack McNally, she was the only girl.

Helen Kovatch is another longtime employee of Frenchtown Elementary School and also worked at the ceramics factory up until it closed its doors in the early 1990s. She attended the high school when it was still in the same building and remembers raising her four children in Frenchtown when "there were at least two hundred kids in the school. You would see kids outside all the time. My son would leave to go play ball in the morning and then be over at the school all day. At night, they would play hide-n-seek for blocks." Kovatch has another unique connection to the school: she delivered her fourth son, Steven, on April 3, 1970, in the ambulance right in front of the building. In fact, baby Steven was delivered by then mayor of Frenchtown, Mayor Ben Cooley.

While families were enjoying the benefits of being part of a tightly knit, safe and self-reliant community, investors saw the opportunity to attract many of those who were relocating to Hunterdon County, as well as visitors and new downtown businesses that would cater to both.

8

TIMES THEY ARE A-CHANGING

1980–2000

While Hunterdon County's population doubled in the decades between 1930 and 1970 and would double again by 2000, Frenchtown's grew at a much slower pace—the number of residents went from 1,459 in 1970 to 1,573 in 1980, though it has declined a bit since then (1,370 in the 2012 census). The county's newcomers preferred new homes on large lots with easy access to major roadways over old homes in towns with aging infrastructure. Developers took note, bypassing the county's older towns and neighborhoods.

Frenchtown's historic features had become a hindrance and weren't espoused to potential newcomers. When Fred Lowe and his wife, Jacquelyn, bought the original home of Frenchtown's founder, Paul Henri Mallet-Prevost, on the corner of Hawk and Railroad Street in 1977, the realtor didn't even mention the home's significance until after the sale. Like many of Frenchtown's dwellings, the previous owner of the Mallet-Prevost House, most likely to be able to afford high property taxes weighing on the borough, had dissected the Mallet-Prevost House—built in 1795 and the oldest house in town—into two apartments. The Lowes had chosen Frenchtown because it was affordable compared to other riverside locales, most likely because the home sat next to an unused railroad track on the edge of a depressed town. In fact, in the late 1970s, the state had officially classified Frenchtown as a depressed rural area.

On the day of the closing on their Frenchtown home, Mr. Lowe walked over to the Warford House (Frenchtown Inn) to buy some beer, and two bikers blocked the doorway, demanding he leave a few bottles behind before they would let him leave. "I doubted my decision in that moment."

Despite the inauspicious welcome, Fred Lowe and his wife were among the town's influx of newcomers who believed in Frenchtown's potential. "We began to see what is referred to today as the gentrification of Frenchtown," explains Lowe. The two were active in the community. His wife became a member of the Frenchtown School Board of Education, and he joined the Frenchtown Planning Board, where he was instrumental in the development and implementation of the town's first master plan for the next ten years.

Newspaperman and author Rick Epstein also moved to Frenchtown in 1977 when he was hired as part-time editor for the *Hunterdon County Democrat*. Soon he was promoted to editor of the *Delaware Valley News* (previously the *Frenchtown Star*), which was based on 207 Harrison Street in the building currently occupied by Frenchtown Chiropractic. The newspaper shared the building with a CB radio shop. Epstein remembers once counting the number of empty storefronts in town—at least half, and the for-rent signs in those were bleached from the sun. "On the upside," says Epstein, "you could give any type of business a whirl because the rent was cheap."

Through his work, Epstein was introduced to Gloria Sipes Paleveda (whose family once owned the *Frenchtown Star*) and edited one of her collection of essays praising the 1930s Frenchtown of her childhood. He also had the privilege of knowing May Ruth Apgar, who was the last of the Apgar family members to reside in the Bridge Street mansion where she lived until her death in her mid-nineties. "She would lend me all the old photos of Frenchtown I wanted to print in the newspaper but would only give them to me one at a time. I visited her often."

Epstein was fascinated with the idea of going back in time and feels fortunate to have glimpsed Frenchtown through the eyes of these two ladies. When he wasn't working, he spent many evenings reading by candlelight on one of the stone piers that hold up the Uhlerstown-Frenchtown Bridge—a pastime security cameras now deter. By the time Epstein moved into his 1800s home at the end of lower Twelfth Street, trains no longer came through Frenchtown, and the only train he ever saw was "the one that came to pick up the tracks."

Frenchtown may have been overlooked by the masses; however, the riverside town still had a certain charm and elegance if one looked beyond the tarnished architecture and faded façades of once grand homes. In the late 1970s, and early '80s, a stroll through the downtown would reveal several of the buildings being dotingly restored.

Henry Sargent Russell was immediately drawn to Frenchtown's understated charm when he arrived on the scene in the late '70s. He and his brother purchased the Gem building as an investment property and

The renovated Gem building as it looked in 2014, viewed from the IOOF Building. *Courtesy of Brokaw Photography.*

family project, and he spent eleven years off and on restoring the magnificent landmark that once housed Frenchtown's talking pictures and a variety store.

Better known locally as Sarge, Russell played a significant role in bringing back Frenchtown's elegant charm, having restored the bars in both the Frenchtown Inn and the National Hotel and built a Tudor home on the Race Street property where the gristmill was located. Perhaps it is because of his unique perspective, having built many fine bars in the county, that he attributes some of Frenchtown's renaissance to the change in the drinking age laws in 1973, when New Jersey lowered the legal age to eighteen, while it remained twenty-one in neighboring Pennsylvania. "Places were hopping along this side of the river, and there was a huge social life in Frenchtown."

Russell also refers to the gentrification that Fred Lowe spoke of—as the predominantly blue-collar town began to see an influx of families, artists and white-collar workers. In his view, agreed to by many others, as the rest of Hunterdon County and points east grew more expensive, Frenchtown benefited.

David Miller, along with a group of investors, purchased the Hummer building on the corner of Bridge and Harrison for $93,000 in 1982. Later,

Above: Henry Sargent Russell's home when he lived in Frenchtown. This view is from Race Street. On the far side of the house is Nishisakawick Creek. *Courtesy of Caroline Scutt.*

Opposite, top: Hummer's Corner in the twenty-first century. *Courtesy of Brokaw Photography.*

Opposite, bottom: John Schmidtberger's painting of Hummer's Corner. *Courtesy of John Schmidtberger and Robert Rando.*

Miller bought out the partnership. When Miller's group took over the building, the space was partially unoccupied—just empty rooms on the second floor and an artist living on the third floor among old ledgers from the Red Men Society and silkscreens left behind by acclaimed artist Allen Saalburg, who had a studio in the space until 1981. Saalburg's illustrations could be found on the covers of *Fortune*, the *Saturday Evening Post* and *Vanity Fair* during the 1920s. His murals hang in the buildings of the parks department in New York City, and some of his later silkscreen prints are on display at the Michener Museum in Doylestown, Pennsylvania.

Miller spent the next twenty-three years restoring the Bridge Street building back to its 1870s splendor, doing most of the work himself. "I really started to like Frenchtown and saw the possibilities. There were so many bastardized buildings that were modernized after World War II without any consideration to the architecture. There wasn't much interest in the historical significance of the town." Miller bought the Victorian house at 112 Harrison—Lois Johnson's childhood home—and spent ten years bringing it back to life. The original house had been built in 1889 for Eloise Hegamen at a cost of $3,000.

"I remember people used to come from New York City to eat at the Frenchtown Inn. They loved the fantastic restaurant in this funky little town with its antique shops and buildings that looked like they were about to fall over. It had a special charm." Frenchtown also caught the attention of the U.S. Department of Housing and Urban Development (HUD), which provided a development grant and low-interest loans that spurred private enterprise.

The empty storefronts filled with antique shops in the mid-1980s. These new entrepreneurs wanted to capitalize on the tourist traffic now coming through Frenchtown on its way to New Hope from the new Flemington Shopping Outlets. The Frenchtown Business and Professional Association, formed in 1979, asked the borough for a stoplight at the end of Route 12 in order to captivate clientele. The mills that once served the area farmers were transformed into upscale apartment and retail spaces. In fact, Blue Fish Clothing, which put Frenchtown on the international fashion scene in the late 1980s, still has its original location in the stone mill building on Route 29. Today, Frenchtown continues to be a draw for clothing designers, and their unique styles can be found in shops on Bridge Street and around the world.

The Frenchtown Historical Society also was convened in the late 1980s. The historical society was short-lived, but its efforts planted the seeds for the Frenchtown Historic District, which was added to the National Register of Historic Places in 1994. Author and architectural historian Ellen Fletcher (now married to Henry Sargent Russell), who moved to Frenchtown in 1990, played a major role in getting the borough listed on the historic register. She moved into 501 Harrison Street and was captivated by the borough's architecture and history. Fletcher then researched 523 of Frenchtown's structures in an effort to understand how the town evolved. "I was intrigued by this river town that had been built according to a plan, unlike other communities that just straggled along the river," she explained. Fletcher was also fortunate to have purchased a home across the street from the Fargo sisters, the daughters of town historian and author Clarence Fargo, and enjoyed hearing their stories of what it was like to grow up in Frenchtown.

The same grant projects that infused Frenchtown with new life also began to change its core, according to Fletcher. "When Harrison Street was widened and parking formalized—taking away trees and grass—the area started to look suburban and the national register requires projects that have any kind of government funding get reviewed for the character of the historic district. If the Harrison Street project had been reviewed, it probably would have been made to look less suburban than it had."

Her extensive research also led to the publication of the most recent book, until now, about Frenchtown, *Sketches of a River Town: A History of Frenchtown, NJ*.

There is one point on which Fletcher's research disagrees with that of Clarence Fargo and other historians. Fletcher never found the name Sunbeam on any map as Fargo referred to in his earlier history of the town. She did find a 1769 map that has Sunbeam on Mount Pleasant because of its eastward facing hill. After endless digging and examination of thousands of deeds, Fletcher concluded that Frenchtown was never officially named Sunbeam.

The romanticism of the name seems to have captured the imagination of Frenchtowners, however, and many locals believe there is more to the name than rumors and are even campaigning to name a new riverside park Sunbeam Park. As one approaches town, whether it is bathed in early morning or late evening sunlight, it is easy to see why Sunbeam is a fitting alternate name, even if it is only a term of endearment.

EMBRACING A NEW MILLENNIUM AND A RICH HISTORY

While the faces in Frenchtown have changed throughout the years, there are quite a few families in the borough and surrounding valley whose roots run deep—Apgar, Dalrymple, Opdyke, Slater and many more. Among them is Robert Elliot Haver II, who has many fond memories of growing up in

Frenchtown in the '80s. He wasn't aware as a young boy of the revolving storefronts—he was only aware that you could get penny candy at Heater's General Store on Bridge Street. He and his wife, Stephanie Markert Haver (also a Frenchtown kid), remember that if you were an upper Harrison kid, you played on Everittstown Hill and if you lived on lower Harrison (closer to the Delaware River), you played in the woods along the river. All the kids knew to stay out of the river. Robert recalls, "There was always something for us to do. Explore along the creek, make up maps of journeys I would take with my dad."

Robert and Stephanie chose to move back to Frenchtown in 2007 when they were ready to have children of their own. They will send all of their four children to the Edith Ort Thomas Elementary School, where they will be the fourth generation of Havers to have gone through kindergarten, not only in the same school but also in the same classroom.

Robert Haver is also a member of the Frenchtown Shade Tree Commission, which dates from the mid-1800s. At his request, the commission recently reinstated handing out seedlings to kids at Frenchtown School, just as they did when he was in school.

None of the Haver children or any others growing up in Frenchtown today will know the pleasure of a bag of penny candy or a free cold drink of water from the Frenchtown Country Well, where five gallons of water will cost you two dollars—still not a bad deal. Fortunately, today's youngsters still have trails along the river and the creek to explore. The first lasting snowfall will bring shrieks of laughter from kids sledding along the same hillside in the Frenchtown Cemetery where many of the borough's children have gone for decades and where many Frenchtowners have made their final resting place.

Another Frenchtown tradition that dates from the turn of the last century and continues today is the Halloween parade. Gloria Sipes Paleveda refers to the parade in all three of her books that feature collections of essays about growing up in Frenchtown in the 1930s. Guy De Sapio remembers that the downtown businesses would have their windows painted by the Frenchtown school kids. "It was exciting because you knew all the kids who painted the windows and the Delaware Valley High School marching band was in the parade."

Today, the downtown comes alive with literary scarecrows made by the Frenchtown School kids—these have become such a popular attraction for visitors and locals that they have been brought to life in several poems, including ones written by Mayor Warren Cooper. Here is an excerpt from Cooper's "Halloween Trick or Treat in Frenchtown, 2010 (4:00)":

Warren Cooper and his bride, Bonnie Pariser, hold court with a papier-mâché bride. The artwork was courtesy of the Frenchtown School. The students present the town each October with a variety of themed papier-mâché creations. *Courtesy of Warren Cooper and Brokaw Photography.*

Piked to the sidewalk, the fourth graders' papier-mâché scarecrows
Slump like dying Christians at the gates of Rome, glaring
At their own blind reflections in shadow-dark shop windows.
Zombies lurch against wind that shreds their paper skin.
Cracked and crenulated limbs tear free and fly across pavement
Or swing like stumps of crash victims. The lost left hand of a
Garish clown, still gripping a bloody rubber axe, bangs against the Launderette door.
Scales of a silver dragon sidewalked on its broad belly outside Schaible's barber shop
Skitter across the pavement to press in leafy piles against Race Street buildings
That lean like headstones. A lone fairy queen, her yellow mop dreds
Snapping about her head, stretches the fingers of one hand
Toward its scarlet-nailed mate lying in the gutter, gusts lifting and twitching
The golden wand with its feeble spell.

Guy De Sapio's family is still strongly connected to Frenchtown and the surrounding valley. De Sapio Construction purchased the Barn Theatre Building in 1996 and remodeled the property into professional office space that now also houses the Secret Garden Montessori School. The building has a unique geothermal water source for heating and cooling and also boasts the borough's first elevator.

When the Barn Theater was being built in 1939, well diggers struck water that gushed to the surface and continues to flow today. For the next fifty years, excess water came out of a metal pipe—now branded Frenchtown Country Well—where it could be drunk or jugged for free by anyone who wanted it before it spilled into a ditch on upper Twelfth Street. The water was used to air condition the theater right up until it showed its last movie in 1989, *When Harry Met Sally*.

Many locals were disappointed to see their beloved Barn Theater transformed into an office complex. Haver remembers seeing *E.T.* and *Spaceballs* at the Barn. His great-grandmother, Nelverna (Eichlin) Bellis, managed the theater. Her husband's name, John Roscoe Bellis, along with the name of his brother, is engraved on the Doughboy Statue that flanks the school. His parents, Jill Elizabeth (Thatcher) Haver and Robert Elliot Haver, are among many long-timers who still live in town.

ALL ROADS LEAD TO FRENCHTOWN

Stroll through Frenchtown today, and you might find a group busily knitting at the yarn shop on Race Street or at the café by the river and cyclists enjoying some ice cream outside of the coffee and bicycle shops that occupy the buildings once home to the silent pictures and the Frenchtown Post Office. Hindi chants float down from the windows of the yoga studio in the beautifully restored Eddy Hardware building, and dogs enjoy a morning run with their owners along riverside paths near the Mallet-Prevost House where gristmills and sawmills used to ring out even as the trains traveled past. Clustered along Bridge Street and fanning out down Race, Front, Harrison and Trenton Streets are a mix of professional offices and clothing boutiques, fine art galleries, a tattoo studio, a bookstore and toy store, salons, a home furnishings and décor store and other specialty shops. The population today may not speak French as a first language, but many of the businesses feature French-themed goods (albeit more focused on French from France than French-Swiss), and it is not uncommon to find a group of Francophiles conversing *en français* over a cup of coffee at the Bridge Café.

There are no longer several barbershops, a butcher or gristmill in town, but staples like a grocery store, a hardware store, a pharmacy and a laundromat are still fixtures in this town, as are the nearby bowling alley and roller rink. The local scene often includes musicians playing on front porches or down by the river, while artists freeze a moment in time on canvas or with a photograph. Frenchtown has long captivated those with an artistic flair. Nathanael West is said to have completed *Miss Lonelyhearts* in a rented room here. Kurt Wiese, known for his illustrations in the original *Bambi* and winner of both the Caldecott Medal and Newbery Award, lived in the Frenchtown area from 1930 until he died in 1974. James Agee, who won the Pulitzer Prize posthumously in 1958 for *A Death in the Family*, lived on Second Street while he was writing the novel. Frenchtown's most well-known resident today is author Elizabeth Gilbert, whose memoir *Eat, Pray, Love* continues to be a source of inspiration for women around the world.

Lisa and Ken Miller converted the old railroad station into the Bridge Café. From the dining room, one can watch those making use of the Rails-to-Trails or catch a good view of the river as it flows past. *Courtesy of Brokaw Photography.*

Top: Local resident Mel and her pup enjoy a walk along the trail that was once a train line. *Courtesy of Brokaw Photography.*

Bottom: The rundown "crooked" buildings on the corner where Bridge Street turns into Race Street. *Courtesy of Brokaw Photography.*

The rickety buildings along this stretch of Race Street were totally renovated in 2014. *Courtesy of Caroline Scutt.*

Frenchtown continues to evolve—from colonial transportation center to early twentieth-century agricultural hub to industrial manufacturing—and today it is the quintessential example of a revitalized small town. In 2012, the borough, which was once referred to as depressed, received the designation of "A Great Place in New Jersey" by the state chapter of the American Planning Association. A year later, the Frenchtown Green Team was awarded a Sustainable Jersey Grant for the town's progress made toward a sustainable future. Most recently, local builder Dorsey Reading received Donald B. Jones Award for Design and Planning from the Hunterdon County Planning Board for his detailed restoration of the iconic crooked buildings on Race Street.

Patrick Henry once remarked, "I know of no way in which to judge the future but by the past." Concerning Frenchtown: What of the future? Wander north along Harrison and up and down the numbered streets, and you will see an eclectic mix of Victorian, Italianate, Craftsman, Saltbox and Bungalows lovingly restored and cared for by residents who, when asked, are proud to share their Frenchtown story, whether it is one that began generations ago or has only just begun.

The renovated, two-story Eddy Building in 2010. *Courtesy of Brokaw Photography.*

There are many festive events in Frenchtown, including Riverfest. One of the events that will entertain both visitors and residents is a pet costume contest, another is the local musicians who take to the stage. *Courtesy of Brokaw Photography.*

The past of Frenchtown contains both historical and romantic interest, but for those who live in the borough these days, everyday life and the cloud-covered future is always a concern. Industries do have a habit of coming and going. At this time, there is no longer train service reaching out to Frenchtown, and the flow of trade down the Delaware is mostly a thing of the past. Nowadays, everyone is connected via satellite or cable, and this offers a glimpse of the type of business that may find a home along the river in the future.

Frenchtown was never a thriving metropolis but rather a nexus allowing for the streaming of businesses in the region while its natural environs and aesthetics keep the river town a magnet. There is a place for Frenchtown in the digital age as industries learn how to flourish by integrating the past with the present in an environment that holds more per capita artists and artisans than most geographic locals within the North American continent.

AFTERWORD

People often ask me how I came to live in this tiny little place called Frenchtown. My joking answer is, "I took a series of accidental left turns, and here's where I turned up." (Which is a pretty good description, actually, of how all of us end up anywhere in our lives.) But the more truthful answer would be love.

About twelve years ago, a month before I went traveling on the journey that would eventually become the basis for *Eat, Pray, Love*, I came out to Stockton, New Jersey, for the weekend to visit two old friends who had recently purchased a house on the river. It was a gorgeous July day, and they took me for a drive around the surrounding villages, hills and farms. I'd never been to this area of the world before, and its beauty staggered me. Also, I felt like I was being let in on some outrageously magical secret. I'd grown up in Connecticut and had lived in and around New York my whole adult life, but I'd never been aware of this gem of a region. All day, I kept saying, "This is here? This has been here the whole time? An hour from New York City? An hour from Philadelphia? Right here? Why doesn't everyone live here?"

I couldn't believe this string of beautiful little towns on the river was so near to everything and yet felt so far away from it all. It was as if I had stumbled upon an American Brigadoon, right in the middle of the Northeast Corridor.

Then my friends took me to Frenchtown, and that was it. I was done for. We had breakfast at the Frenchtown Café—an establishment that appeared to have been untouched since about 1948. We wandered through the little shops, where the owners spoke to us personally and warmly. We walked along the bike path with its dappled leafy light and strolled across the bridge. Standing in the middle of the bridge—on that wavering dividing line between Pennsylvania and New Jersey—I looked north up the river and saw…nothing. Nothing but water, trees and sky. We could have been in the middle of Vermont, for how pristine that view was. Ducks flew overhead, fish swam underneath and a fantastic ice cream cone was available at the Bridge Café only steps away…what else could a girl want?

I was about to go spend a year traveling around the world, but I made a quiet mental note that day, which went like this: "Here. When the time comes someday to settle down, it will be here."

It would be another four years before I could finally make good on that promise, but I did it. By the time I came back to Frenchtown, I had a new husband with me, and together, we started a business and settled into the flow of this community. It was a good move for us. I loved it here every bit as much as I had suspected I would.

I always say that my favorite thing about Frenchtown is that it's built on a human scale—that everything is within a walkable reach, and everyone's lives are in such close physical proximity to one another. This place is the very opposite of suburban sprawl and urban isolationism. You know how there are such things as bedroom communities? Well, Frenchtown is a sidewalk community. Most everything of importance in this town is solved on a sidewalk because neighbors see one another in real time every single day—passing one another on the way to school, to work, to the post office. All the news of Frenchtown is exchanged standing up, face to face, under a shade tree or a street lamp, with a coffee cup in one hand and a dog leash in the other. Kids run from backyard to backyard, free-range and fully at ease. The local police slow down their cruisers to gently tease the teenagers on their skateboards, and the kids tease the cops right back. If you lose a cat, chances are your neighbor will find it in her garage and return it by sundown. If you find a cat, odds are that you'll know whose cat it is right away. If you don't recognize the cat, your neighbor on the other side—the one who's lived here for seventy-five years—will. (She knew that cat's great-great-great-grandmother, for heaven's sake; she would be able to identify those markings anywhere.)

I have learned in Frenchtown both the beauties and the perils of small-town living. There are dramas that unfold here, just like anywhere else, but our dramas often get magnified (paradoxically) by the smallness of this place. When I first moved to town, I asked an old-timer, "What's the business of Frenchtown, anyhow?" He smiled, and warned me, "Other people's business, honey. So watch your back."

To be sure, there are no secrets here (I swear, I've found out things about myself from other people before I even knew them), and stories can sometimes grow big and crazy in the fishbowl that is our little community. Another old neighbor of mine put it this way: "You stub your toe on Second Street, and by the time the news reaches Eighth Street, they'll be saying you had your leg amputated."

But I don't mind. I prefer this small-town gossip mill to the scarier big news of the outside world. I like that when your fire alarm goes off because you overcooked your pot roast, it's your friendly neighbor Mike who swings by from the fire department to make sure everything is OK. I like that when somebody suffers an illness or loss, the neighbors rally with baskets of food and support for the family. I like that things are so quiet here when somebody steals spare change out of another person's car it's a huge breaking story, on par with Chappaquiddick. Those are the kind of stakes I can deal with. And the flip side of all that gossip and intrigue is this: when you're in trouble, they are always there for you. And by "they," I mean "everyone." And when you have something to celebrate, they will celebrate with you as well.

When my husband and I first opened our import business here in town, we had a four-ton marble Buddha statue (imported from Vietnam—don't ask!) that needed to be carried up Bridge Street and placed in front of our building. The only problem is, the flatbed truck carrying the Buddha was way too big and way too long to make the corner without shutting down traffic. And you aren't legally allowed to shut down traffic on Bridge Street. Unless, of course, you have a parade permit—as Mayor Sworen reminded us, with a twinkle in his eye.

So we applied for a parade permit, and we ended up throwing a Buddha-moving parade! Every kid in town followed the flatbed truck as it made its way slowly through our village. The kids threw streamers and flowers and danced around, banging on buckets and grooving with hula hoops. As we passed by every house, residents came out, regarded the spectacle with curiosity and then unquestioningly joined the march. (They didn't even know what all the commotion was about, but it must have looked like fun, and Frenchtowners are always up for spontaneous fun.) By the time we and our neighbors and our giant Buddha made it to our new building, the parade had turned into a full-out party.

A stranger to town that day watching the festivities as the large white marble Buddha slowly sailed up Bridge Street said to our police chief, "I've never seen anything like this in my life."

Chief Al just smiled and tipped his hat. "Well that's how we do things here," he said.

And that's why I live in Frenchtown.

Because it's the best.

Elizabeth Gilbert

BIBLIOGRAPHY

Beers, F.W. *Atlas Map of Hunterdon County*. New York: Beers, Comstock & Kline, 1873.

Fargo, Clarence B. *History of Frenchtown: With Interesting Sidelights on Surrounding Communities*. New York: Clarence B. Fargo, 1933.

Fletcher, Ellen. *Sketches of a River Town: A History of Frenchtown, NJ*. Hunterdon County, NJ: D.H. Moreau Books, 1997.

Johnson, Bruce. *Covered Wooden Grandstands*. N.p.: self-published, 2012.

Nathanael West. Pamphlets on American Writers 21. University of Minnesota, 1962.

National Park Service. "Frenchtown Historic District Hunterdon NJ." National Register of Historic Places Continuation Sheet. NRIS Reference Number: 94000438, 1994.

Paleveda, Gloria Sipes. *The Best of Times: Memories of the Delaware Valley*. Philadelphia: Better Baby Press, 1986.

———. *A Fond Look Back*. Hunterdon County, NJ: Frenchtown Historical Society, 1984.

———. *I Remember: A Fond Look Back at Life in the Delaware Valley*. Hunterdon County, NJ: D.H. Moreau Books, 1997.

Pearson, William W. *Frenchtown Up to Date: Growth and Development of the Borough, Leading Firms and Business Men*. N.p.: self-published, 1916.

Race, Henry. "The First Years of Frenchtown." *Jerseyman* 2, no. 1 (1893): 22–5.

———. "The West Jersey Society's Great Tract in Hunterdon County." *Jerseyman* 3, no. 1 (April 1895).

Schmidt, Hubert G. *The Press in Hunterdon County, 1825–1925*. Flemington, NJ: Democrat Press, 1961.

———. *Rural Hunterdon: An Agricultural History*. New Brunswick, NJ: Rutgers University, 1946.

Seiden, Max. *Frenchtown Centennial Program, 1867–1967*. Hunterdon County, NJ: Democrat Press, 1967.

Shafer, Mary. *Devastation on the Delaware: Stories and Images of the Deadly Flood of 1955*. Ferndale, PA: Word Forge Press, 2010.

Snell, James P., and Franklin Ellis. *History of Hunterdon and Somerset Counties, New Jersey with Illustrations and Biographical Sketches of the Prominent Men and Pioneers*. Philadelphia: Everts & Peck, 1881.

Union National Bank. *Ninety-sixth Anniversary, Union National Bank of Frenchtown, NJ, 1856–1952*. Booklet. N.p., 1952.

Whitehead, William A. *East Jersey Under the Proprietary Governments: A Narrative of Events Connected with the Settlement and Progress of the Province, Until the Surrender of the Government to the Crown in 1703*. Newark, NJ: M.R. Dennis, 1875.

INDEX

S

T

U

W

ABOUT THE AUTHORS

All roads lead to Frenchtown. For author, mother, volunteer and social entrepreneur Caroline Scutt, that statement is true on many levels. Several years ago, she decided to change her life course and found herself in Frenchtown. She quickly fell in love with this offbeat, eclectic community. She now calls Frenchtown home and lives here with her husband, Jeff; daughter, Julia; and a house full of furry family members.

Ms. Scutt began her professional writing career in 1992 as a reporter for *Travel Weekly* newspaper and has since authored articles on an array of topics for various print and online outlets. She published her debut novel, *Some Girls*, in 2013.

When she isn't writing or helping build a stronger community through her work at United Way of Hunterdon County, she can be found sharing her love for stories at her shop, The Book Garden, in Frenchtown, New Jersey.

Ms. Scutt is actively involved in her local community and is a recently elected member of the Frenchtown Borough Council. She holds a master's degree in medical humanities from Drew University.

Dr. Robert F. Rando began his career as National Research Council fellow at the Centers for Disease Control in Atlanta, Georgia. Over the years, he has lived in various states in the United States and in a province in Canada, traveled extensively, managed drug discovery and development programs, written patents and published his work in peer-reviewed scientific journals.

At the beginning of this century, he and his family (his wife and two children) moved to Hunterdon County and put down roots; this is also when the fiction bug bit him. His first fictional work was published in 2006. He is now a proud co-owner of The Book Garden. Recently, another challenge emerged: the Frenchtown area needed an updated treatise covering its history. Dr. Rando no longer writes about advances in molecular genetics, as his interests instead focus on local history, social anthropology (fiction) and producing the *River Town Radio Theatre*, which airs on WDVR in Sergeantsville, New Jersey.